YOU CAN TRUST

100 DEVOTIONS
TO ANSWER YOUR WHAT-IFS

FOR B

BY KATY BOATMAN

B&H
PUBLISHING GROUP
Brentwood, Tennessee

For my nephew, Blake. May you always know
that God will never leave your side, and He
can fight every scary thing you are thinking
about. I love you so much, buddy!

Published by B&H Publishing Group,
Brentwood, Tennessee

978-10877-8749-7

Dewey Decimal Classification: J242.62
Subject Heading: DEVOTIONAL LITERATURE / BOYS / CHRISTIAN LIFE

Unless otherwise noted, Scripture quotations are taken from the Christian Standard
Bible®, Copyright © 2017 by Holman Bible Publishers. Used by permission. Christian
Standard Bible® and CSB® are federally registered trademarks of Holman Bible
Publishers, all rights reserved. Scripture references marked ESV are taken from the
English Standard Version. ESV® Text Edition: 2016. Copyright © 2001 by Crossway
Bibles, a publishing ministry of Good News Publishers. Scripture references marked NIV
are taken from the New International Version®, NIV® Copyright ©1973, 1978, 1984,
2011 by Biblica, Inc.® Used by permission. All rights reserved worldwide. Scripture
references marked NIRV are taken from the New International Reader's Version, copyright
© 1995, 1996, 1998, 2014 by Biblica, Inc.®. Used by permission. All rights reserved
worldwide. Scripture references marked NLT are taken from the New Living Translation,
copyright © 1996, 2004, 2015 by Tyndale House Foundation. Used by permission of
Tyndale House Publishers, Inc., Carol Stream, Illinois 60188. All rights reserved.

Cover Illustration by Hannah Tolson.

1 2 3 4 5 6 7 • 27 26 25 24 23

CONTENTS

Before You Start Reading 1

Question 1: What If I Have a Lot of Questions? 4

Question 2: What If I Don't Feel Strong Enough? 6

Question 3: What If I'm Scared? 8

Question 4: What If My Team Loses? 10

Question 5: What If I Don't Know If I Can Trust God? 12

Question 6: What If It's Not Fair? 14

Question 7: What If I Don't Want to Get Out of Bed? 16

Question 8: What If I Fail? 18

Question 9: What If I Embarrass Myself? 20

Question 10: What If Something Scary Happens at School? 22

Activity Day/Answer Recap 24

Question 11: What If God Gives Up on Me? 26

Question 12: What If I Don't Know What's Coming? 28

Question 13: What If I Can't Be Still? 30

Question 14: What If I Have a Nightmare? 32

Question 15: What If No One Takes Me Seriously? 34

Question 16: What If I'm Waiting on an Answer? 36

Question 17: What If I'm Afraid of the Dark? 38

Question 18: What If Everything in My Mind Is Swirling? 40

Question 19: What If I Want to Hide? 42

Question 20: What If I Don't Want to Be Patient? 44

Activity Day/Answer Recap 46

Question 21: What If I Don't Know How to Pray? 48

Question 22: What If I Don't Make My Parents Proud? 50

Question 23: What If I Feel Left Out? 52

Question 24: What If Everything Is Too Loud? 54

Question 25: What If I Get It Wrong? 56

Question 26: What If I Need Forgiveness? 58

Question 27: What If a Crime Hurts My Family? 60

Question 28: What If It's Going to Hurt? 62

Question 29: What If God Stops Loving Me? 64

Question 30: What If I Get Sick? 66

Activity Day/Answer Recap 68

Question 31: What If Someone Doesn't Respect Me? 70

Question 32: What If I Get Bored? 72

Question 33: What If There's Too Much to Get Done? 74

Question 34: What If I Can't Decide? 76

Question 35: What If I'm Too Young? 78

Question 36: What If I Can't Fall Asleep? 80

Question 37: What If No One Sees Me? 82

Question 38: What If I'm Nervous for the First Day? 84

Question 39: What If I Don't Want to Ask for Help? 86

Question 40: What If I Get in a Fight? 88

Activity Day/Answer Recap 90

Question 41: What If They're Better than Me? 92

Question 42: What If I Don't Have What I Need? 94

Question 43: What If I'm Trying to Stay Out of Trouble? 96

Question 44: What If I Can't Wait? 98

Question 45: What If God Can't Hear Me? 100

Question 46: What If My Stomach Hurts Because I'm Nervous? 102

Question 47: What If I Don't Want to Cry? 104

Question 48: What If Things Don't Get Better? 106

Question 49: What If I'm Scared of a Disaster? 108

Question 50: What If I Get Overwhelmed? 110

Activity Day/Answer Recap 112

Question 51: What If I Hate Tests?............................114

Question 52: What If I Can't Keep Up?.......................116

Question 53: What If I'm Not Sure What's True?...............118

Question 54: What If Following the Rules Is Hard?.............120

Question 55: What If I Keep Messing Up? 122

Question 56: What If the News Is Scary?......................124

Question 57: What If I Don't Know When to Pray? 126

Question 58: What If I Don't Have All the Information?..........128

Question 59: What If I'm Worried About Tomorrow?............130

Question 60: What If I Oversleep? 132

Activity Day/Answer Recap..................................134

Question 61: What If I'm Different Than My Family? 136

Question 62: What If My Parents' Jobs Change? 138

Question 63: What If I Can't Get All A's?......................140

Question 64: What If I Want People to Like Me?...............142

Question 65: What If I Have a Bad Day? 144

Question 66: What If Everything Is Changing? 146

Question 67: What If Something Happens to My Family?..........148

Question 68: What If I'm Not as Good at Everything?............150

Question 69: What If I'm Scared to Talk to God? 152

Question 70: What If I'm Tired of Being Brave? 154

Activity Day/Answer Recap..................................156

Question 71: What If I'm Dreading Something? 158

Question 72: What If I'm Alone? 160

Question 73: What If My Feelings Are Hurt?...................162

Question 74: What If I Get Homesick?.......................164

Question 75: What If I Can't Fall Asleep?.....................166

Question 76: What If I'm Disappointed?.......................168

Question 77: What If My Feelings Are Out of Control? 170

Question 78: What If I'm Nervous? 172

Question 79: What If Everything Is Too Serious? 174

Question 80: What If I Disagree with Someone? 176

Activity Day/Answer Recap 178

Question 81: What If I'm Scared of Storms? 180

Question 82: What If I Don't Want to Grow Up? 182

Question 83: What If the Next Step Is Hard? 184

Question 84: What If I'm Scared to Ask God? 186

Question 85: What If I Made a Big Mistake? 188

Question 86: What If I Hate That My Body Is Changing? 190

Question 87: What If I Can't Calm Down Before God? 192

Question 88: What If God Changes His Mind About Me? 194

Question 89: What If People Don't Like Me? 196

Question 90: What If I Have to Stand Up for What I Believe In? 198

Activity Day/Answer Recap 200

Question 91: What If Heaven Is Not Real? 202

Question 92: What If I Don't Matter? 204

Question 93: What If I Can't Stop Thinking About It? 206

Question 94: What If It's Not What I Planned? 208

Question 95: What If I Regret Something? 210

Question 96: What If I Don't Want to Be Honest? 212

Question 97: What If God Isn't Who He Says He Is? 214

Question 98: What If I'm Too Excited to Sleep? 216

Question 99: What If the Worry Lasts Forever? 218

Question 100: Can I Trust? 220

Activity Day/Answer Recap 222

Index 223

Thank You 232

Before You Start Reading

I know you have a lot of questions about the way things work.

How many times have you woken up with your mind full of questions, swirling with all the "what-ifs"? You think about each thing that went wrong the day before, the things you are nervous about for tomorrow, and everything you're scared of as the day gets started! Before you know it, your mind is moving so fast you can't keep up with it, and now you're worried, mad that you're worried, and mad at everything in general.

God knows and understands everything on your mind—all the things you're upset and worried about—and He's there to help you fight those things. He sees and hears all those worries and what-ifs that are distracting you at school, making you anxious, and keeping you frustrated and angry.

These one hundred devotions won't tell you how *everything* works, but they will help you understand a lot more about how *God* works. You'll realize that He can be trusted, and He will never give up on you. And if you choose to read a devotion each morning, you can start your day thinking about how much God loves you. After every ten devotions, there is an activity for you to do. These are fun, interactive ways to help you apply what you have been reading.

When you finish all one hundred devotions, I pray you know and remember these things:

God is not scared.

God will fight for you.

God is always working.

God has answers for all your "what- if" questions.

God is who He says He is.

God is always with you.

And you can trust Him.

You will keep the mind that is dependent on you in perfect peace, for it is trusting in you.—Isaiah 26:3

A Note About Asking Adults for Help

As we talk about things that worry you and all the questions on your mind, I want you to know it's okay to reach out to adults who can help, such as doctors, counselors, pastors, teachers, and parents! Some worries and problems are too big to handle alone. Some of the topics we're going to talk about in this book may be an overwhelming issue for you and something that reading a short devotion can't help solve. If you're battling those things or dealing with a diagnosis of anxiety or depression, it is absolutely okay (and necessary) to ask for help. No one is supposed to carry these anxieties alone. You are so loved.

QUESTION 1

WHAT IF I HAVE A LOT OF QUESTIONS?

"Call to me and I will answer you and tell you great and incomprehensible things you do not know."—Jeremiah 33:3

Like all kids, your mind is full of questions. You have questions about how the world works. You have a lot of "what-if" questions. You have questions about God. Maybe you have questions about what's going to happen this coming year. Or perhaps your questions are about why certain things happened in the past.

God is not scared of all the questions you have. In fact, He welcomes them!

Just as a soldier has questions for his commander about what his task is, you have questions for God. And that is completely fine!

Following God requires trust, and God works in big ways that our human minds sometimes can't understand. (This is true for adults too.) You can ask God anything you want. The best resource we have is the Bible, which is God's Word. It's like your manual for life. You will find a ton of answers and examples when you read the Bible. Don't be intimidated by how long it is! It's full of stories of how God kept His word, His purpose for your life, and what He's promised for all the days ahead.

You won't find every answer to every question in the Bible, but you will discover what God has chosen to reveal about Himself, humanity, and life itself. The more you study it, the more truth you'll discover—just ask any grown-up who's been a Christian for a long time!

Don't allow those questions to keep you from getting to know God. Try writing them all out on paper and then praying about them. Bring them all to God—your questions about the world, your future, and your family. Even if you don't get an answer, He has a plan. The Bible shows all of us that God has never failed, and He won't fail you either.

You can trust God.

ANSWER

GOD DOESN'T GET ANNOYED BY YOUR QUESTIONS. IN FACT, HE LOVES THEM. YOUR CURIOSITY IS WELCOMED, AND HE WANTS TO HEAR ALL ABOUT IT.

QUESTION 2

WHAT IF I DON'T FEEL STRONG ENOUGH?

The Lord will always lead you, satisfy you in a parched land, and strengthen your bones. You will be like a watered garden and like a spring whose water never runs dry.—Isaiah 58:11

Have you ever broken a bone before?

If you have, then you know that suddenly your plans change for the days ahead when the doctor gives you the news you don't want to hear: "You need to wear this cast/boot/sling for six weeks."

The minutes on the clock start to slow down as you wince in pain, wondering how much longer it will take for your bones to heal. How much longer will it be before you can go back to playing flag football with your friends? Or swim? When will your bones be strong again?

You probably feel strong when you're able to pick up something heavy or do something hard without crying. But did you know that true strength comes from God?

The Bible tells us God will make our bones strong (Isaiah 58:11).

It says God heals the brokenhearted and heals their wounds (Psalm 147:3).

God renews our strength when it's gone (Isaiah 40:31).

On the days when you don't feel strong enough (whether it's your bones or your mind), spend time with God. Remember that your strength comes from Him and that He is all-powerful, with the strength to do anything, anywhere, anytime. When you trust God to be who He says He is, you might quit holding back tears and realize it's okay to let them out. You might quit trying to build strength on your own.

You can allow God to heal you. You can pray about every emotion and share it with God. You can be strong, because He is your strength.

You can trust God.

ANSWER

YOUR STRENGTH COMES FROM GOD, WHICH IS THE BEST NEWS! IT MEANS YOU DO NOT HAVE TO PROVE YOURSELF. IT'S EXPECTED THAT YOU WON'T FEEL STRONG AT TIMES, BUT GOD WILL ALWAYS COME THROUGH.

QUESTION 3

WHAT IF I'M SCARED?

"When you pass through the waters, I will be with you, and the rivers will not overwhelm you. When you walk through the fire, you will not be scorched, and the flame will not burn you."—Isaiah 43:2

Do you like haunted houses or spooky movies? I am not a fan! They are at the top of my list of things I'm scared of.

What's at the top of your list of fears? Maybe it's spiders. Or going to a new school. Or facing that bully.

We all have things that set off our fears, no matter how old we are. But God tells us over and over again in the Bible not to fear. It's not because He doesn't care about our feelings. It's a reminder that He is in control and we are not. What a relief!

Now, you may read today's verse and think that God's people never get hurt or that He always makes life easy. But you have to remember to look at the Bible as a whole story and not just individual verses. There are plenty of times in Scripture when God's people were hurt or suffering (like in the book of Job). The people in the Bible were scared a lot too, and God did not promise to take away those scary things. Instead, He promised us *Himself*. That's the gift!

If you read all Isaiah 43, you see just how many scary things God was prepared to rescue His people from. And that's still true today. When you are scared, He is your safe place (Psalm 46:1). He is your shelter from the storm (Isaiah 4:6). He is your protector and fortress (Psalm 18:2). You can trust in Him (Psalm 145:19).

You may not be passing through water or fire like it says in today's verse, but no doubt you have lots of scary things going on around you because there is lots of sadness and sin in the world! And whatever you named on your list of fears does not have to be the first thing on your mind today.

God has called you by name. He is whispering, "Hey, I know you're scared, and that's okay because You are mine. I've got this."

You can trust God.

ANSWER

YOU HAVE A PROTECTOR IN GOD, AND YOU ARE NEVER ALONE!

QUESTION 4

WHAT IF MY TEAM LOSES?

A fool gives full vent to his anger, but a wise person holds it in check.—Proverbs 29:11

I recently was watching my nephew, Blake, play flag football. His buddy, Kyle, is also on his team, and the two make a great duo. Their team is pretty good too. They get along well on and off the field, and they really hustle during the game.

But this team just can't seem to win a game. Football season has been frustrating for them because they keep finding themselves up against teams they can't seem to beat. You've probably heard the saying, "It's not whether you win or lose, it's how you play the game." Or "It's not about who wins or loses, it's about having fun." Those sayings might be true, but they don't take away the sting of a loss.

The reality is, your team is going to lose sometimes. It might be your own soccer, hockey, or basketball team, your favorite college football team, or the NFL team you've been rooting for since birth. Any time two teams play against each other, though, one team will lose. There's no way you're going to win them all every single time. So the question shouldn't be: *What if my team loses?* The questions should be: *What do I do when I lose? How do I handle it?*

It's okay to be sad or disappointed or frustrated, but it's important you know what to do with those feelings. Don't become rude or take your frustration out on other people. You can say you're mad or sad, but you have to keep moving forward and work toward trusting that you will get another shot next time. As today's verse reminds us, fools let out their anger, but wise people keep their anger under control.

Every game is a fresh start, just as every day is a "new mercy," as the Bible tells us. Another game is a brand-new challenge. Another tournament is a blank page. Another day is a gift.

The next time your team loses, what if you tried saying one of these:

"We lost today. I'm sad, but it's okay. I'll keep practicing and try again next time."

"I'm disappointed we lost. I need a minute to be sad, but it's going to be okay."

"I'm frustrated we lost, but I want to thank you for coming to watch me play."

You can trust God.

ANSWER

LOSING IS GOING TO HAPPEN SOMETIMES, BUT IT DOESN'T DEFINE WHO YOU ARE OR HOW GOOD YOU ARE. GOD DEFINES THAT.

QUESTION 5

WHAT IF I DON'T KNOW IF I CAN TRUST GOD?

Take delight in the LORD, and he will give you your heart's desires. Commit your way to the LORD; trust in him, and he will act, making your righteousness shine like the dawn, your justice like the noonday.—Psalm 37:4–6

Just for a minute, think about walking over a small creek in the woods. Have you ever come up on one and noticed a large log or wooden plank you could use to cross over the water? What do you do before you step onto the log or plank? I bet you take one foot and tap on it to make sure it's sturdy enough to hold you. Before you walk on it, you want to know if you can trust it, because if it's not strong enough, you'll fall.

Sometimes, you might wonder if God is strong enough for you and if He can be trusted. How do you know you can trust Him when you can't see Him? How do you know you can trust Him in those moments when everything around you feels hard and scary?

To get our answer, we turn to the Bible, God's Word, to learn more about who He is and what He does.

- The book of Genesis says that God created you and the world you live in. You can trust the One who created you (Genesis 1:1, 27).

- God can always be trusted because He promised a Savior would come to save the world, and Jesus did (Isaiah 9:6–7).

- God can always be trusted because He gives you the Holy Spirit to live with you and be your Helper (John 14:26).

- God can be trusted because He is a good Father. He never fails you (Romans 8:15).

- God can always be trusted because over and over in the Bible, He says He's going to come through for us, and He does (Joshua 21:45).

Although other people in your life might let you down, you can trust God.

ANSWER

YOU CAN TURN TO THE BIBLE TO PROVE THAT GOD HAS ALWAYS KEPT HIS WORD.

QUESTION 6

WHAT IF IT'S NOT FAIR?

May grace and peace be multiplied to you through the knowledge of God and of Jesus our Lord.—2 Peter 1:2

Someone else getting picked for the team. Your brother getting to sit in the front seat instead of you. Not getting the dog you've been begging for. Losing the game to your biggest rival. It's not fair, right? It stings, it's not fun, and it's not what you want!

I could just say, "Life's tough and not fair," and move on, but I want to be a better friend to you than that. Let's talk about what to do with all the emotions when things don't feel fair. Because the reality is, there will be a lot of moments when things just aren't right.

It can be really easy to let the frustration and anger take over, and although it's okay to admit that things aren't as you want them to be, there is one response I want you to choose in those moments: kindness and compassion.

God knows things aren't as they should be, and that's why He sent His Son, Jesus, to die on a cross for you, to make right what you couldn't. But while you're here on this earth, all the broken pieces of life are still hard to navigate. Some days the things that don't seem fair are small, like losing the video game you're playing. Other days the things that don't seem fair are big, like finding out you have to move to a new school. In either case, God can help you navigate what you're feeling.

Responding with kindness when things don't feel fair seems like the opposite of what you really feel (mad), but you can ask God to help you. Other people will see the love of God through your actions, and you don't have to rely only on yourself to get over your frustration. God can work in you and through you.

You can trust God.

ANSWER

ASK GOD TO HELP YOU MAKE SENSE OF YOUR FEELINGS AND RESPOND WELL. EVEN WHEN YOU'RE MAD, GOD CARES ABOUT THAT TOO.

QUESTION 7

WHAT IF I DON'T WANT TO GET OUT OF BED?

He will not allow your foot to slip; your Protector will not slumber. Indeed, the Protector of Israel does not slumber or sleep. The LORD protects you; the LORD is a shelter right by your side. The sun will not strike you by day or the moon by night.—Psalm 121:3–6

This morning I woke up, and it was cold and snowing outside. I had a full to-do list of things that needed to be done, a few phone calls I was not looking forward to, and zero desire to get out of bed. Everything sounded hard, but my bed sounded cozy and easy.

Have you ever had a morning like this? Have you woken up and thought you'd rather stay in bed than face what's ahead that day?

We often think the day is going to be too much or too tiring or too hard. And we believe we've got to be strong enough and good enough to do it all, without asking for help.

Do you remember the song "He's Got the Whole World in His Hands"? Sometimes you might sing along to a song like this, just like you do to your favorite song from a movie, without paying attention to what the song means. But the words tell us that God is holding the world—everything around us—carefully in His hands. Think about the last time you held an egg in your hand. I bet you were pretty careful with it, making sure it didn't break until you were ready for it to. God holds the world with care, and you are safe in His hands.

When you're nervous to get your day started because you don't want to face what's ahead, you have to remember God carries the world, including what you're about to face. He is Almighty God, and as Psalm 121 tells us, He is always working. You don't have to stay in bed to make sure everything will be easier. It's all in God's hands, and He wants to handle it for you.

You can get up. You can start the day.

You can trust God.

ANSWER

THE BIBLE TELLS US THAT GOD GOES BEFORE US (DEUTERONOMY 31:8). WHATEVER YOU DON'T WANT TO FACE TODAY, HE'S ALREADY THERE, CARRYING IT FOR YOU.

QUESTION 8
WHAT IF I FAIL?

I am sure of this, that he who started a good work in you will carry it on to completion until the day of Christ Jesus.—Philippians 1:6

Do you ever hesitate to start a new project or try a new thing because you're afraid you might fail? It's like standing at the bottom of a climbing wall and deciding not to climb because you're sure you can't make it to the top.

Think about that climbing wall for a second. As you stand at the bottom, staring at the bell you need to ring at the top, you have different paths to choose from, but you do have climbing grips to hold. You may not get there on the first try. You may not even get there at all, but you have support, an opportunity to try, and a chance to learn from your mistake if you put your foot in the wrong place.

God already knew you would fail over and over again, which is why He sent Jesus to take on your sin. So take the pressure off yourself! Failure is normal, and if you let the idea of it stand in your way, you miss out on a lot of incredible chances to learn and live. The gift in it all is that you can choose to trust the climbing holds—the handles you have in God. He is your support, your path, and your guide.

Failing at something does not define who you are. God defines who you are, and as today's verse reminds us, He will complete a good work in you (Philippians 1:6)!

You can trust God.

ANSWER

IT'S OKAY TO FAIL AT SOMETHING. IN FACT, IT'S NORMAL AND EXPECTED THAT YOU WILL! IT DOESN'T CHANGE THE WAY GOD SEES YOU. TRUST IN THE FACT THAT HE'S NOT GOING TO WALK AWAY.

QUESTION 9
WHAT IF I EMBARRASS MYSELF?

"You are the light of the world. A city situated on a hill cannot be hidden. No one lights a lamp and puts it under a basket, but rather on a lampstand, and it gives light for all who are in the house."
—Matthew 5:14–15

The first time I was asked to sing a solo in my school's choir, I was terrified. *What if I forget the words? What if my voice cracks? What if my friends don't think choir is "cool"? What if I embarrass myself in front of everyone?*

You can come up with every reason why you might not look good in front of other people. You can often keep yourself from experiencing something really fun, only because you think you might mess up or you're just afraid to draw attention to yourself in general.

But remember this: you are awesome. Want to know how I know that even though I've probably never met you? God made you. And God makes really cool things.

Feeling like you look bad in front of others may happen from time to time, but it doesn't mean it's true of who you are.

Try that new thing. Be okay with embarrassing yourself every now and then. Be confident in how God made you and the unique interests He gave you.

And you know what? If there's a day when you just feel stuck thinking about what everyone is thinking of you and you don't feel good enough, let me remind you that God lives in you. That's the coolest part of a relationship with Him! You're walking around on earth with the King of the world living in you. He's your Father, Helper, and Friend, and His light shines through you. That can't be ignored.

You can trust God.

ANSWER

WHEN YOU GET EMBARRASSED, BRUSH IT OFF. GOD ONLY MAKES GOOD THINGS.

QUESTION 10

WHAT IF SOMETHING SCARY HAPPENS AT SCHOOL?

In every situation take up the shield of faith with which you can extinguish all the flaming arrows of the evil one.—Ephesians 6:16

I remember being in college when a tornado touched down really close to our campus. Thankfully, my house and school buildings did not get hit by the tornado that night, but trees, branches, and power lines covered the yards and streets, making the walk from home to class much trickier than the day before.

We watched the news to see areas of town where the storm had done more extensive damage and sat there feeling sad for the people who lost their homes while also feeling grateful that we were safe.

It's strange to feel both ways at the same time.

Have you ever experienced a mix of feelings when you heard about something scary happening at a school? Maybe you were scared, angry, confused, or you were relieved it wasn't you. Or maybe something scary has happened at *your* school. How did it make you feel? Has it made you nervous it will happen again?

These feelings can make a classroom no longer seem as safe as it once did. Will that story on the news be your story too?

When scary things happen, it's sometimes easy to wonder where God is in those moments. But you know the answer! He lives in you.

Call His name. Ask for strength. Ask for a calm mind. Ask Him to remind you every single second of the school day that He's with you. And pick up the "shield of faith" as the Bible says (Ephesians 6:16). Whenever something feels scary or overwhelming, God is your defender. He's not going to leave.

You can trust God.

ANSWER

GOD IS YOUR PROTECTOR AND DEFENDER. HE WILL BE RIGHT THERE WITH YOU WHEN YOU'RE SCARED OR FACING SOMETHING SCARY. YOU ARE NEVER ALONE.

ACTIVITY DAY

Which day in these ten days did you read about the "shield of faith"? (Hint: It's from Ephesians 6:16.)

Find a cardboard box, poster board, or cereal box you're about to recycle, and use it to create your own shield.

Use your creation as a physical reminder that you are armed with a shield of faith.

ANSWER RECAP

- God loves your questions. Your curiosity is welcome, and He wants to hear all about it.

- Your strength comes from God. You won't feel strong at times, but God will always come through.

- You have a protector in God, and you are never alone!

- Losing doesn't define who you are or how good you are. God defines that.

- You can turn to the Bible to prove that God has always kept His word.

- When life's not fair, ask God to help you make sense of your feelings and respond well.

- Whatever you don't want to face today, God is already there, carrying it for you.

- It's okay to fail at something. It doesn't change the way God sees you.

- If you get embarrassed, brush it off, because God only makes good things.

- God is your Protector and Defender. He will be right there with you when you're scared or facing something scary.

QUESTION 11

WHAT IF GOD GIVES UP ON ME?

In him you also were sealed with the promised Holy Spirit when you heard the word of truth, the gospel of your salvation, and when you believed.—Ephesians 1:13

Have you ever tried to get your dad's attention while you're in a grocery store, but no matter what name you called him, he was so focused on finding the perfect bananas that he didn't hear you? *"Dad! Daddy! Bill! Hey!"* Eventually, you probably just gave up and waited for him to realize that even though you were pushing the cart toward the cereal aisle, you had already thrown in your favorite with the marshmallows.

As funny as that can be, I think we sometimes can feel this way about calling out to God. *Is He there? Did He hear me?*

Maybe you're afraid that you have forgotten about God one too many times, so He's going to forget about you. Or you're scared you have messed up one too many times, and He is staying mad at you. Maybe you still have a lot of questions about Him, and you're worried that's going to annoy Him.

Humans have a limit to what we can handle, so we often think God does too. But He doesn't have a limit. God will always recognize your voice and not give up on you. The Bible shows us one example after another of people who continuously let God down, yet He never turned away from them:

- When Abraham messed up again and again, God didn't give up on him. He built a nation through Abraham's family.

- When Moses messed up again and again, God didn't give up on him. He used Moses to help lead His people to freedom.

- When David messed up again and again, God didn't give up on him. In fact, it was through David's family line that Jesus was born.

God is faithful and true to His Word. He will hear your prayers and keep showing up for you.

You can trust God.

ANSWER

GOD WILL ALWAYS BE THERE FOR YOU. HE WILL NEVER GIVE UP ON YOU OR CHANGE HIS MIND ABOUT YOU. HE LOVES YOU SO MUCH, NO MATTER HOW YOU FEEL ABOUT HIM.

Question 12

What If I Don't Know What's Coming?

Our Lord is great, vast in power; his understanding is infinite.
—Psalm 147:5

When's the last time you went somewhere new? Maybe it was a new doctor's office or the first time going to guitar lessons. Maybe it was a concert or a football game at a big stadium.

Does going somewhere new make you nervous?

I like to know what to expect. If I'm heading to a concert at a place I've never been, I want to know where I'm supposed to park, how bad traffic will be, if I should eat before I go, if the crowd will sit or stand the whole time, and how long the concert will last. (I know, I have a lot of questions.) That's how I prepare my mind for what's to come.

On the morning when you're heading somewhere new, are you like me? Do you think about all the things ahead? Sometimes I can get so caught up in this that I become afraid when I *don't know* what's coming. It's just like riding a roller coaster! Before I get on, I want to see what twists and turns to expect, but often you just can't see all the crazy turns while standing in line.

When I start to fear what's next, I remind myself that God is all-knowing. This means He already knows what happened yesterday, what happens today, and what will happen tomorrow. I can remain calm, because even if I don't know what's coming, He does. Also, I trust Him. He's never failed me.

And think about this: Because the Bible tells us the whole story of God's creation, we already know how things will end. There will be a day when Jesus returns to earth, and you'll get to spend forever with God. So you don't know everything that's coming, but you do know you get to spend the future with God, the One who is all-knowing! And that's your hope—forever with Him.

You can trust God.

ANSWER

YOU MAY NOT KNOW WHAT'S COMING, BUT GOD DOES. FOLLOW HIM. STICK WITH HIM. HE WILL GUIDE THE WAY.

QUESTION 13

WHAT IF I CAN'T BE STILL?

"Be still, and know that I am God. I will be exalted among the nations, I will be exalted in the earth!"—Psalm 46:10 ESV

Playing hide-and-seek is a ton of fun, but the being still and quiet part is a little tough when you're alone, hovering in the corner of a dark closet, hoping you win the game. It's as if the stillness brings on a new level of uncomfortable, and now both your mind and legs are squirming.

Can you think of another time you needed to be still when you felt like it was impossible? You probably didn't even realize you were not being still until someone let you know!

Although being still might feel like a punishment, it is often a chance to focus and hear or see something we may not see otherwise. Think about it like this: When you're out on a walk and you come across a bug or animal you want to see more closely, what do you do? You don't start running toward it, making a lot of noise! You get quieter. You stand still. You make as little noise as possible so you don't startle the creature and can get a better look.

The next time you need to be still, what if you think in a similar way? What's waiting for you in the stillness that you need to see or hear? What if you started to pray in those moments? What if you asked God to show you what you're supposed to see and hear?

When your body wants to go, go, go, or your mind is distracted by noises or spiraling thoughts, God is there to help calm your outside and your inside. Being still is not a punishment; it's a moment to pause, take a deep breath, and rest.

It's a moment to accept God's offer of peace and calm.

You can trust God.

Answer

Remember that being still isn't a punishment. Sometimes it's an invitation to pause, calm down, and be with God.

QUESTION 14

WHAT IF I HAVE A NIGHTMARE?

"The LORD will fight for you."—Exodus 14:14

Think about your favorite superhero for a second. Is it Spider-Man? Black Panther? Batman?

The fun of watching a movie about superheroes is getting to cheer them on as they fight. You know they're powerful because you've seen them battle the bad dudes and win, so you trust that they'll come out on top no matter what.

Did you know that when you face hard battles, God fights for you?

Let's think about nightmares for a second. They can be the worst. If you wake up after having one, your heart might still be racing as you try to figure out what's real and what's not. In those moments, the first thing you can do is start praying. Ask God to calm you down and remind you He's fighting for you.

God can fight the nightmares. Let Him.

If you're too worried to fall asleep because you're scared you're going to have a nightmare, here are some verses to read and think about when it's time for bed:

When you lie down, you will not be afraid; you will lie down, and your sleep will be pleasant.—Proverbs 3:24

Don't be afraid of them, for the LORD your God fights for you. —Deuteronomy 3:22

One of you routed a thousand because the LORD your God was fighting for you, as he promised.—Joshua 23:10

No matter who or what distracts you, scares you, or tries to stand in your way, Jesus wants to be with you. Your dreams and your life are safe with Him. You don't need a superhero. You have the God of the universe, and He will fight for you.

You can trust God.

ANSWER

LET GOD FIGHT THE NIGHTMARES FOR YOU. ASK HIM SPECIFICALLY TO PROTECT YOUR SLEEP AND YOUR DREAMS. IF YOU DO HAVE A BAD DREAM, YOU CAN ASK HIM TO HELP YOU CALM DOWN AND FALL BACK ASLEEP. NOTHING IS TOO SMALL OR TOO BIG FOR HIM.

QUESTION 15

WHAT IF NO ONE TAKES ME SERIOUSLY?

Then David said, "The LORD who rescued me from the paw of the lion and the paw of the bear will rescue me from the hand of this Philistine."—1 Samuel 17:37

Have you heard the story of David and Goliath? David was a young shepherd, which meant his job was to watch over the sheep—and sheep aren't very clever. They need to be watched over.

One day a Philistine soldier named Goliath showed up to battle the Israelites. Goliath was nine feet, nine inches tall. A giant! His size was so intimidating that no one wanted to fight him.

David was young and small, and no one took him seriously, but God doesn't care how young we are. He can work through anyone. David took one rock and a slingshot and was able to defeat Goliath! The small shepherd boy, whom everyone doubted, won the battle with God on his side.

Do you ever feel like people don't take you seriously because of your age?

No matter how old you are, you have an important part to play in the world and in the kingdom of God. I learn so much from watching your generation navigate your faith and relationship with Him. In fact, it's a reminder to me that sometimes I overcomplicate it all.

As you continue to get to know the Bible and discover more about who God is, don't be afraid to share it with other people. You are not too young for God to work through. Many adults can learn from the way you focus on loving God well instead of figuring out all the ins and outs about Him.

As someone who is young, you are important to the work of God on this earth, even if you don't know how to navigate all the things that feel so big.

You can trust God.

ANSWER

REMEMBER THAT YOU MATTER TO GOD AND PLAY AN IMPORTANT PART IN THE WORK OF HIS KINGDOM! YOU ARE NOT TOO YOUNG OR IMMATURE TO TELL OTHER PEOPLE ABOUT HIM.

QUESTION 16
WHAT IF I'M WAITING ON AN ANSWER?

In the morning, LORD, you hear my voice; in the morning I plead my case to you and watch expectantly.—Psalm 5:3

When's the last time you had to wait to get an answer to something big? Maybe you were waiting to hear if you made the basketball team or waiting for your grade after taking a test you studied hard for. Maybe you were waiting on some results from a doctor or waiting to hear if your mom got a new job that will require her to travel more.

When we're excited or scared about the possibility of something that may or may not happen, we can get worked up in the waiting.

Will I make the team?

Will I get the part?

Will they let me play?

Do we have to move?

Will I get what I want?

All the waiting can make us nervous and squirmy and irritated. It's like we're stuck in the doctor's office waiting room without any game or device or TV to distract us from thinking about what's to come.

Here's something we can learn while we wait: whether the answer is *yes*, *no*, or *maybe*, God's plan is always better than our own.

It's okay to be sad if you don't get what you want, but God is teaching you something while you wait, and He's teaching you something with the way He answers. His plans for you are good, whether you can see it right now or not. And when you ask Him for something, remember that no matter the answer, He always offers you love, joy, peace, patience, kindness, goodness, faithfulness, gentleness, and self-control in the middle of it (Galatians 5:22–23). God always has something good for you in the waiting because that is who He is.

You can trust God.

ANSWER

NO MATTER WHAT THE ANSWER IS, GOD HAS A PLAN FOR THE WAITING AND A PLAN FOR HOW IT ALL PLAYS OUT. AND HE IS WITH YOU WHILE YOU WAIT.

Question 17

What If I'm Afraid of the Dark?

Even the darkness is not dark to you. The night shines like the day; darkness and light are alike to you.—Psalm 139:12

Have you ever been camping or out in the backyard during a very dark night? It's crazy just how dark it can get. You might not be able to see your friend who is just a few feet away, and you have no idea what else is out there with you.

When I am trying to sleep at night, I leave a small light on so I can still distinguish everything in my room. I don't like the dark because I can't see anything.

Our minds sometimes come up with crazy ideas in the darkness. When we can't see, we often react to what we think is there. We imagine scary things in the shadows. We wish we could shine some light in the darkness.

Whether you're camping out on a dark night, or in a dark room trying to fall asleep, or the darkness is something you're feeling inside, let me tell you the truth about darkness:

God can see in the dark, and He is not afraid of it.

Today's verse tells us that darkness is just as light as daytime to God. That means He knows where you should step when walking in the dark *and* He knows what's coming your way in the future, which you can't see.

Whatever kind of darkness is scaring you, ask God to shine some light on it. Ask God to make it brighter. And remember that even if you still can't see in the dark, He can.

You can trust God.

ANSWER

WHAT IS DARK IS NOT ACTUALLY DARK TO GOD. RELY ON HIM TO BE YOUR LIGHT AND YOUR EYES WHEN YOU CANNOT SEE.

Question 18

What If Everything In My Mind Is Swirling?

They will be called righteous trees, planted by the Lord to glorify him.—Isaiah 61:3

Have you ever spun around so many times you got dizzy and couldn't walk straight? The Dizzy Bat Race game is the funniest way to see this happen. Each player places his forehead on the end of a baseball bat, holds the bat to the ground, and then spins around until he's dizzy. Then the participants have to try to race to the finish line. Typically, everyone starts running in weird directions or falling because they can't seem to figure out how to run straight.

Sometimes life can feel out of control like this, and you can't see straight. Maybe you and your parents are trying to make a decision about what school to go to next year. Maybe you're waiting to find out about your dad's job and if your family has to move. Maybe someone in your family is really sick, and there's nothing you can do to help. Whatever the case, sometimes it feels like everything is changing around you, yet you're left standing in the middle, spinning out of control.

In another translation of the Bible (NIV), today's verse refers to God's people as "oaks of righteousness." Do you know why I like that phrase? An oak is a tree that's tall and firm and steady. Its branches may sway in the wind, but it stands tall.

I love this reminder that if we are planted by the Lord, our tree roots are in *Him*. The unshakable and steady One. The One who can't be torn down.

So when you feel like a tree being blown around in the wind, when you feel like your life is spinning out of control, when you feel like you're too dizzy to even see straight, remember where your roots are: in the unmoving, unfailing love of God. He is not surprised by the changes, and He will continue to hold you steady with every move ahead.

You can trust God.

ANSWER

GOD CAN STEADY ALL THE THOUGHTS IN YOUR MIND. HE IS YOUR SAFE PLACE.

QUESTION 19

WHAT IF I WANT TO HIDE?

"Can a person hide in secret places where I cannot see him?"—
the Lord's declaration. "Do I not fill the heavens and the earth?"—
the Lord's declaration.—Jeremiah 23:24

My dog likes to hide under my bed when I start getting dressed and ready for the day. He knows it's a sign I'm going to leave him. He thinks he's sneaky, but I can always see his tail sticking out from under the bed. The little dude can't get away with much with such a big, fluffy tail.

It makes me think about the days I wish I could hide under my bed too. How many times would I run there because I was scared? How often would I head into that hiding place when I knew I'd messed up and didn't want anyone to find me?

We may not be able to hide under our beds, but we do hide a lot, don't we? Sometimes we hide what we're feeling because we don't want to talk about it. Sometimes we hide what we've done because we know it was wrong. And sometimes we hide who we are because we think no one will like us.

But here's the thing: you cannot hide from God. That might seem intimidating, but it's actually a wonderful invitation to come to God with whatever— yes, *whatever*—you're feeling. He already knows!

Nothing you will do (or have already done) will change the way God feels about you. When He looks at you, He's delighted. When He thinks about you, He smiles. His love for you is bigger than any mistake you've made, and it's stronger than your deepest fear.

Underneath the bed you try to hide beneath, God is waiting to remind you that you are seen and loved at the very same time.

You can trust God.

ANSWER

GOD WILL MEET YOU IN YOUR FAVORITE HIDING SPOT, BUT HE ALSO WILL TEACH YOU IT'S OKAY NOT TO HIDE AT ALL. HIS LOVE FOR YOU IS BIGGER THAN THE THING MAKING YOU WANT TO HIDE.

QUESTION 20

WHAT IF I DON'T WANT TO BE PATIENT?

A patient person shows great understanding, but a quick-tempered one promotes foolishness.—Proverbs 14:29

*P*atience. It's not a word I much care for. Do you? When someone's telling me to be patient, or I know I'm in a situation when I need patience, it means there's something I desperately want but don't have yet (like waiting for a fun vacation to start). Rather than wait, I want it *now*. Can you relate?

You don't want to wait for dinner to be ready. You don't want to wait to find out if you got the part in the school play. You don't want to wait for your dad to get home from his work trip. You don't want to wait until your friend returns from summer camp.

You're ready to eat. To perform. To see your dad. To hang with your friend. You're ready. Why isn't the rest of the world?

The Bible talks a lot about patience. Patience is a choice; it's something we adjust in our attitude. It is uncomfortable, but it helps us grow. With the Holy Spirit's help, we are capable of choosing patience, even when we don't automatically feel it.

In the book of Job, we read about a man who is going through one hard thing after another. He loses his family, is covered with sores all over his body, and loses his animals. He could have easily freaked out and lost his cool (and no one would blame him), but he instead kept worshiping and waiting on God. Can you imagine the patience and self-control it took to wait on God's timing?

God always has a plan. When you have a hard time waiting, you can ask Jesus to give you both the patience and strength to wait calmly. He lives in you, remember? He's strong enough to carry your burden of waiting.

You can trust God.

ANSWER

THANKFULLY, GOD CAN HELP. PATIENCE DOESN'T ALWAYS COME EASILY, BUT YOU HAVE A HELPER IN THE HOLY SPIRIT, WHOM YOU CAN CALL ON WHEN YOU KNOW YOU CAN'T BE PATIENT ON YOUR OWN.

ACTIVITY DAY

Find a stick or bat you can use to play the Dizzy Bat Race game mentioned in Question 18, and go play that game outside near a tree.* If you can't find a tree around, play it near something that you can lean on and will be steady (like a pole or the side of your house).

After you spin around ten times with your forehead on the top of the bat, try to run and see what happens. When you need something to lean on, lean your hand on the tree or steady object you found and say, "God is my steady, safe place."

Use this as a reminder that when everything feels too crazy, we can lean on our steady God.

*Safety check: Don't forget to make sure you have enough wide-open space to spin without hitting anything else, and clear away any rocks or branches so that you don't trip!

ANSWER RECAP

- God will never give up on you or change His mind about you.

- You may not know what's coming, but God does. Follow Him. Stick with Him. He will guide the way.

- Remember that being still isn't a punishment. Sometimes it's an invitation to pause, calm down, and be with God.

- Ask God specifically to protect your sleep and your dreams. Nothing is too small or too big for Him.

- You are not too young to matter to God and play an important part in the work of His kingdom!

- When you're waiting for an answer, remember that God has a plan. And He is with you while you wait.

- What is dark is not actually dark to God. Rely on Him to be your light and your eyes when you cannot see.

- God can steady all the thoughts in your mind. He is your safe place.

- When you want to hide, God will meet you in your favorite hiding spot, but He also will teach you it's okay not to hide at all.

- Patience doesn't always come easily, but you can call on the Holy Spirit to help when you know you can't be patient on your own.

QUESTION 21

WHAT IF I DON'T KNOW HOW TO PRAY?

This is the confidence we have before him: If we ask anything according to his will, he hears us.—1 John 5:14

When you open a new Lego set, are you the type of person who likes to follow the instructions on how to put it all together, or do you just go with the flow and figure it out on your own?

We're all different in the way we approach things like that. Some of us need a step-by-step process, and some of us would rather tackle the project without the instruction manual.

When you think about praying to God, does it feel like you need instructions?

It's easy to start thinking there's a formula to praying—that you have to speak in a formal way or say things in a particular order. The truth is, God wants you just to talk to Him. He is your Creator and Father, so He deserves honor and respect as you approach Him, but He also wants you to tell Him everything as you would your closest friend.

And guess what? He hears every word, and He knows your voice!

When you're worried about praying correctly, it can lead you not to pray at all. So don't overthink it. Spend time with God like you would spend time with your best buddy. Talk to Him. Listen for Him. Thank Him. The more you do, the closer you'll grow to Him and the more confident you'll be in your prayers.

He knows the questions and worries swirling around in your head, because He made you, and it means you're not left alone to figure out those worries. He's not a God of confusion (1 Corinthians 14:33). If nothing seems clear to you, everything is clear to Him. As you pray, let Him lead the way.

You can trust God.

ANSWER

WHEN YOU PRAY, GOD'S NOT LOOKING FOR YOU TO HAVE ANY FANCY WORDS OR SPECIAL SAYINGS. HE JUST WANTS YOU TO TALK TO HIM.

QUESTION 22

WHAT IF I DON'T MAKE MY PARENTS PROUD?

But you are a chosen race, a royal priesthood, a holy nation, a people for his possession, so that you may proclaim the praises of the one who called you out of darkness into his marvelous light.—1 Peter 2:9

When I was around six years old, I slipped and fell after coming off stage at a choir performance. I held it together until I got back to my seat with my parents, and then I started tearing up. I wasn't crying because I was hurt; I was crying because I was embarrassed. I was embarrassed for me and for my parents. Were they embarrassed too?

It feels really good to be complimented and affirmed by your parents and teachers and mentors. You want to hear nice things about what you did or said and how you performed. You want to know if your parents saw your accomplishments and noticed when you got better at something, made a good grade, or did something kind for someone.

But in the moments when you think you've disappointed or embarrassed your parents, you can easily get really down on yourself. You start beating yourself up over what you could have done differently, and you get mad at yourself and sometimes everyone around you.

But what you mean to God is not based on anything you can or cannot do. You are valuable because you belong to God. You can be strong because God gives you strength. You can do great things because He will work through you.

All of us have days when we trip up and mess up. But making your parents or anyone proud of you isn't something you have to stress over, because you were created by a God who only makes good things. He's proud of you just because you're His.

You can trust God.

ANSWER

YOU MAKE GOD PROUD, AND IT'S NOT BECAUSE OF ANYTHING YOU'VE DONE. IT'S BECAUSE OF WHO YOU ARE.

QUESTION 23

WHAT IF I FEEL LEFT OUT?

"What do you think? If someone has a hundred sheep, and one of them goes astray, won't he leave the ninety-nine on the hillside and go and search for the stray?"—Matthew 18:12

Have you ever felt left out? Maybe you didn't have a partner for the class project or your neighborhood friends started a game of flag football and didn't invite you.

The feeling of being left out burns. It can make you feel mad, anxious, and lonely. You wonder what you could have done or said differently so that you would've been included. You might even make a long list in your mind of all the things that are wrong with you.

But being left out of fun plans doesn't mean you are not loved. It simply means sometimes humans forget about other humans. It means sometimes people are selfish and don't think about other people's feelings. It means sometimes friends let you down.

Whenever I feel lonely or left out, I try to remember an important truth about God: He is our Shepherd. Now, this may feel like a strange thing to think about because we don't see shepherds around anymore. But a shepherd's job is to watch and know what his sheep need. In Matthew 18:12, Jesus tells a story about a shepherd who has one hundred sheep, but one of them gets away. The man doesn't hesitate to leave the ninety-nine other sheep to go find the one that went missing! In the same way, God will come find you. You are never alone or forgotten.

If you have recently been left out, or you don't have a friend to hang out with, or you feel like no one sees you, remember, *God will come looking for you*. He attends to His sheep. You're not invisible to Him.

You can trust God.

ANSWER

GOD IS ALWAYS WITH YOU. WHETHER YOU ARE FEELING LONELY IN YOUR ROOM OR WATCHING A GAME OF KICKBALL THAT YOU WEREN'T INVITED TO PLAY, HE'S NOT FORGOTTEN YOU OR LEFT YOUR SIDE.

QUESTION 24

WHAT IF EVERYTHING IS TOO LOUD?

"Don't let your heart be troubled. Believe in God; believe also in me."—John 14:1

When's the last time you attended a big football or basketball game? If you haven't had a chance to go to a game yet, which sport would you like to see in person, and which team would you cheer on?

I am a big Georgia Bulldogs fan, and I love getting the chance to go to a game. It's so much fun to cheer along with all the other fans and see the action in person instead of on TV!

But live sports are loud. When you try to ask the person next to you a question, there's a good chance he won't hear you because of all the noise.

Does your mind ever feel this loud inside? Sometimes problems are swirling around in our heads so much—worries about our schoolwork or our team or middle school—that our thoughts get so loud we can't possibly hear or understand ourselves.

When this happens, here's an idea: find a quiet space—in your room, under a tree outside, on your porch—and work out what you're feeling on the inside. Bounce a ball, hit a punching bag, draw until the marker is dry, or do some jumping jacks. It might feel weird or uncomfortable, but just give it a minute! Even consider writing down what's going through your head. The physical act of putting thoughts on paper or moving your body can help the loud, jumbly mess inside your head become something you can let go of.

And most of all, tell God everything. Spill it out. All the noise inside your mind doesn't have to take over your day. Bring God the things that cause all the noise. The trouble in your heart and the trouble in your mind are not troubles to Him. He can turn down the volume and bring you peace.

You can trust God.

ANSWER

TURN THE VOLUME DOWN BY GETTING STILL AND QUIET FOR A BIT. ASK GOD TO HELP CALM ALL THE THINGS THAT SEEM TO BE "SCREAMING" SO THAT YOU CAN HEAR HIM BETTER.

QUESTION 25
WHAT IF I GET IT WRONG?

He uses his powerful word to hold all things together.
—Hebrews 1:3 NIRV

I've been out of school for many, many years, and I still think spelling bees are terrifying. Whose idea was it to make kids stand in front of a room full of people and spell words out loud for everyone to hear? If you love a spelling bee, I am impressed, because it all just makes me nervous. First, I'm trying to concentrate on seeing the word in my head, then spelling it correctly out loud, then wondering what everyone is thinking as I spell, and especially what they're thinking if I get it wrong.

Do you get nervous about getting something wrong?

Maybe instead of getting nervous you get angry whenever you give the wrong answer or make the wrong decision. We can get ourselves really worked up over wrong moves, and it can be for so many reasons! Sometimes we just can't stand to be wrong. Sometimes, we're trying to impress other people. Other times, we've tried so hard to get it right that we're exhausted from trying. *What if I just get it wrong again?* Even talking about the what-ifs makes us a little tired.

Take a deep breath. It's okay to be wrong sometimes, and it's okay to work really hard at studying for a spelling bee or a test and still getting the answers wrong. It's going to happen! You're not perfect even when you want to be.

But that's why God is the coolest. He knew you couldn't be perfect, in big ways and small ways. He knew you'd need Him. He sent Jesus to rescue you! He's always there with you to remind you that everything will be okay. Getting something wrong doesn't change the world because God's holding the world.

You can trust God.

ANSWER

IF YOU GET SOMETHING WRONG, IT DOES NOT CHANGE THE WORLD, AND IT DOES NOT CHANGE GOD. YOU'RE GOING TO BE WRONG SOMETIMES, AND THAT'S OKAY.

QUESTION 26

WHAT IF I NEED FORGIVENESS?

Confess your sins to one another and pray for one another, so that you may be healed. The prayer of a righteous person is very powerful in its effect.—James 5:16

Not too long ago, I watched a little buddy build a tiny Lego city. It had people and cars and a fire truck. But as I watched him get close to finishing, I saw the terror on his face as he saw his little brother running full speed toward the Lego city. Maybe the two-year-old would stop, maybe he would sit down and help, but I could tell by the crazy look in the toddler's eye that helping was not his plan. He crashed right into the tiny city of Legos, ruining his big brother's work.

It was all chaos from there: pushing, shoving, some crying and yelling. Feelings were hurt, everyone was angry, and the Lego city was no longer a city.

One thing I wish I had known more about when I was younger was *forgiveness*. We will all make mistakes and hurt each other's feelings because we're all messy and imperfect (it's why Jesus came to save us!). But when you've hurt someone or gotten really angry when you didn't mean to, what can you do?

As today's Bible verse says, you can go to the person and tell them you're sorry. Ask them to forgive you, and say, "I was wrong for taking out my anger on you." Pray for them, and ask God to forgive you as well. I know that can be hard and sometimes awkward, but it will be worth it to strengthen your relationship with that person and with God.

And you know what? God will forgive! Just as an eraser wipes away the words on a white-board, God can wipe away your mistakes (1 John 1:7). This wiping away is called forgiveness, and God is very good at it.

You can trust God.

ANSWER

THERE IS NOT A THING GOD WON'T FORGIVE YOU FOR. YOU ARE IN GOOD HANDS.

QUESTION 27

WHAT IF A CRIME HURTS MY FAMILY?

Pray at all times in the Spirit with every prayer and request, and stay alert with all perseverance and intercession for all the saints.—Ephesians 6:18

I know today's topic is a little heavy, but I also know when you see a glimpse of the daily news or you watch a movie with a scary scene, it puts real ideas in your head about all the "what-ifs" that could happen to you or your family too. So let's talk about one of those things.

No one likes to think about being the victim of a crime, but I know seeing a crime in real life or on TV might keep you up at night.

First, take time to realize that very often your fear of crime comes from seeing made-up stories on TV. But whether it's a movie that has you scared or something real you saw on the news, talk to your parents about your fears, and work together on some practical safety steps for your family. Having a plan for what to do if you see a crime or how to call for help if something happens at home can make you feel less scared. Now, let's talk about another important step.

Pray. Prayer can be a weapon. Did you know that? James 5:16 says, "The prayer of a righteous person is very powerful in its effect." It's your way of fighting against darkness and evil in the world. You take it to God! If you're having trouble falling asleep or you're scared to be home alone, pray! It sounds like such a small thing to do, but it has a mighty impact. Pray that He will help those who are hurting. Pray that God will keep your family safe. Pray for a peaceful, calm heart.

The God who created you is strong and powerful, and He's your protector. He's with you in your fear, but He also wants to take it away. He can surround your home and your family with an armor of protection.

You can trust God.

Answer

GOD DOES NOT DISAPPEAR WHEN THINGS GET SCARY. HE IS WITH YOU, FIGHTING FOR YOU, LISTENING FOR YOUR VOICE. USE PRAYER AS A WEAPON. TAKE DEEP BREATHS, REMEMBERING THAT GOD IS YOUR SAFE PLACE.

QUESTION 28

WHAT IF IT'S GOING TO HURT?

The LORD will protect you from all harm; he will protect your life.
The LORD will protect your coming and going both now and forever.
—Psalm 121:7–8

No one likes getting a shot at the doctor's office. Even though the prick of a needle is typically quick, all we can think about before it happens is how much it's going to hurt. The last time I was at the doctor I didn't have to get a shot, but I found out at the last minute that I had to get blood drawn. This was probably for the best, because I didn't have time to start worrying about it!

Sometimes you know something painful is coming, whether physical or otherwise. Maybe your friend is moving at the end of the school year, or you're going to have surgery soon. Maybe you're leaving one school to start over at a new one, or maybe one of your parents is moving out of your house. Whatever it may be, it can leave you dreading the pain to come.

God knows it all, though. He knows what it will be like, and He will not leave you to go through any of it alone. As everyone tells you to be strong and brave, remember where your strength and bravery come from—God! Just like a superhero can do hard things because of his superpowers, you can do hard things because of God's power. Trust that He will carry you through it.

As you watch the nurse prepare your shot or your friend pack up to move, look for signs of God, like a game of "I Spy." He's in the nurse's smile, your friend's fist bump, and the deep breath you take to stop the tears. But it's okay to admit it hurts. Jesus is with you.

He's the best person to run to. Our Protector. Our Healer.

You can trust God.

ANSWER

GOD CAN TAKE AWAY YOUR PAIN. HE CAN BRING YOU COMFORT AND PEACE WHEN YOU'RE HURTING. TELL HIM WHAT HURTS.

QUESTION 29

WHAT IF GOD STOPS LOVING ME?

The faithful love of the LORD never ends! His mercies never cease.
—Lamentations 3:22 NLT

We get really used to things running out. Your favorite cereal is gone within a few days. The toilet paper roll is empty once again. The light bulb eventually burns out. We even know the feeling of other people running out of patience with us when they get frustrated or annoyed.

Can I tell you one of the greatest things about God? His love will never run out.

Imagine standing on the side of a river and watching the water flow downstream. God's love is like that; it flows and flows for you and never runs dry.

Yes, things in our life will come to an end. Church camp is over in a week. Friendships fade. And sometimes our parents even get divorced (if this is you, I just want to say how very sorry I am that you are facing this hardship). Thankfully our verse today reminds us that "the faithful love of the LORD never ends!"

God loves what He made, and He especially loves you! Even if life has been hard or overwhelming or frustrating lately, God has not changed His mind about you. He is not going anywhere; in fact, He has had a loving plan for your life even before you were born.

So, today, as you start your day, thank God for His love. It is not based on what you did yesterday or what you will do tomorrow. His love is here to stay.

You can trust God.

ANSWER

GOD IS A GOD WHO STAYS. THERE IS NOTHING YOU CAN DO THAT WILL CHANGE HIS LOVE FOR YOU. ISN'T THAT INCREDIBLE NEWS?

Question 30

What If I Get Sick?

Be gracious to me, Lord, for I am weak; heal me, Lord, for my bones are shaking.—Psalm 6:2

Are you afraid of getting sick?

Whether it's a cold, or COVID-19, or cancer, no one wants to get sick. There's so much unknown attached to all of it. Being sick also means missing out on things. Maybe spending one day with no schoolwork and watching a movie isn't so bad. But when one day turns into one week, you start missing your friends, your routine, and having fun. You wonder, *How far behind with classwork will I get? Is there a party I will miss? What if I have to go to the hospital?*

It's normal for your brain to have these questions, but because of Jesus, you have the power to pause and pray. After all, spending the time and energy on what-ifs will only make you more tired and more stressed out.

So do your best to stay healthy and take care of the body God has given you. You know what to do: get enough sleep, eat healthy food, and wash your hands well. And if you do wake up with a fever or find yourself sick, God will still be everything you need. Here are some truths to remember:

- God is a healer (Jeremiah 30:17). He can take away the pain.

- God is a sustainer (Psalm 54:4). He can carry you through all the symptoms when you feel like you don't have the strength.

- God is your Father (Matthew 6:9). He will be right there with you when you don't feel well.

- God is a provider (Philippians 4:19). He can bring the right doctors and medicines to you to help.

- Jesus came to heal the sick, not the healthy (Mark 2:17), and He can handle anything.

You can trust God.

ANSWER

YOU KNOW THE BEST DOCTOR THERE IS: THE GREAT PHYSICIAN! IF YOU GET SICK, YOUR GOD CAN HEAL YOU AND HOLD YOU TIGHT.

ACTIVITY DAY

Push-up challenge! See how many push-ups you can do in thirty seconds while you recite this verse from Question 28 out loud:

> The LORD will protect your coming and going both now and forever.
> —Psalm 121:8

Hate push-ups? Try sit-ups or jumping jacks!

ANSWER RECAP

- When you pray, God's not looking for fancy words or special sayings. He just wants you to talk to Him.

- You make God proud, and it's not because of anything you've done. It's because of who you are.

- When you feel left out, God is always with you. He's not forgotten you or left your side.

- When life feels loud, ask God to help calm all the things that seem to be "screaming" so that you can hear Him better.

- If you get something wrong, it does not change the world, and it does not change God. You're going to be wrong sometimes, and that's okay.

- There is not a thing God won't forgive you for. You are in good hands.

- When things get scary, God is with you, fighting for you, listening for your voice. Use prayer as a weapon.

- God can take away your pain. He can bring you comfort and peace when you're hurting. Tell Him what hurts.

- God is a God who stays. There is nothing you can do that will change His love for you.

- You know the best doctor there is: the Great Physician! If you get sick, your God can heal you and hold you tight.

QUESTION 31

WHAT IF SOMEONE DOESN'T RESPECT ME?

"Blessed are the peacemakers, for they will be called sons of God."—Matthew 5:9

Have you ever felt like someone was disrespectful to you? Maybe you're not even sure what that word really means yet, but you know the feeling when someone doesn't believe you, or makes fun of you, or embarrasses you on purpose in front of other people. The feeling can give you a pit in your stomach and then make you wonder how many other people might treat you that way.

So what do we do in those moments? Let's think about what Jesus did. In the Bible we can read about so many times when people didn't believe who He said He was. He was yelled at, spit on, harassed, and betrayed (Matthew 26). None of it was acceptable or fair, but Jesus knew God had a purpose and plan through it all. Every time, Jesus chose peace. He chose humility. He knew His worth and strength and power came from His Father, God, and so does yours.

If someone is disrespectful to you, stand up for what is right and true. Jesus did. But remember that your actions and words matter in those moments too. It takes a lot of self-control to choose love and peace and humility when you feel like you're being treated unfairly, but you're capable of it because God lives inside us when we are Christians. And what He knows, and what you need to know too, is that someone else's bad behavior often has more to do with the hurt they're feeling inside than anything you've done. Allow God to handle their heart and their hurt. And He'll handle yours too.

You can trust God.

ANSWER

PEOPLE ARE JUST MEAN SOMETIMES. CHOOSE TO BE KIND, AND DON'T ALLOW HURTFUL WORDS OR ACTIONS TO DEFINE WHO YOU ARE. GOD DEFINES WHO YOU ARE.

QUESTION 32
WHAT IF I GET BORED?

I don't say this out of need, for I have learned to be content in whatever circumstances I find myself.—Philippians 4:11

Do you hate being bored? I'm guessing that being bored is one of your least favorite things, and "I'm bored!" might be one of your mom or dad's least favorite things to hear!

In today's world we can be constantly connected. At the first hint of boredom, some sort of device is often within arm's length to rescue us. And if not, the boredom can feel heavy and like some sort of punishment. We might feel disconnected and unsure of what to do with the down time.

But did you know that God never meant for your mind to be full of constant noise and busyness? Did you know that moments of boredom are a great time to dream, to create, to think, to pray? Instead of immediately getting irritated that you're bored, think of it as a chance to get creative.

The next time boredom strikes, pay attention to what's around you. Notice the people. Whom could you talk to? Pay attention to what you have around you. Grab some sticks or empty boxes and build something. Get a notebook and write a song, a story, or the rules for a new game. Go on a walk, or work on your sprints or handstands.

Boredom can offer a little more quiet and a little more stillness so your mind can refuel. Use the quiet around you to dream up new ideas. If you focus on being bored, you'll be bitter about things you can't do. But if you focus on the simple things around you, you'll learn to celebrate what you have.

This celebration of what you have is called being *content*. It's an invitation to be grateful. The next time you're bored, ask God to show you all that you have, and choose a thankful heart instead of an unhappy one.

You can trust God.

ANSWER

USE BOREDOM AS A CHANCE TO USE YOUR MIND AND GET CREATIVE. GOD GAVE YOU A BEAUTIFUL WORLD AND SMART BRAIN. USE THE EXTRA TIME WISELY!

QUESTION 33

WHAT IF THERE'S TOO MUCH TO GET DONE?

Whatever you do, do it from the heart, as something done for the Lord and not for people, knowing that you will receive the reward of an inheritance from the Lord. You serve the Lord Christ.
—Colossians 3:23–24

Even if school comes easy to you, homework can be stressful. Some days you have plenty of time to get the work done, and other days you have baseball practice, your sister's play, and a giant project due the next day. You wonder how you will get it all done.

This overwhelmed feeling can leave us anxious—paralyzed trying to figure out what to do next—and stressed before we barely start our day. In fact, I felt that when writing this book. It has brought so much joy to my life, but knowing I had to meet deadlines left me worried about my time and fearing I couldn't get everything done.

These anxious moments are going to come and go in your life, so the best thing to do when they happen is to pause for a moment. Stop thinking about *all* the things you need to do. Instead, identify one best next step and do that. Then, trust God with the step after that and the step after that.

Ultimately, God is not concerned with how many things you checked off your to-do list. He's more concerned with your attitude and your faithfulness while you do them.

Also, you can ask for help when you need it! Sometimes boys feel pressure to be so strong that you think you aren't allowed to ask for help, but that's not true. A teacher, a parent, or a friend can help you figure out what to do next and remind you of what matters along the way.

I pray before I write each one of these devotions. I want these words to be from God and not from my own head. I want to trust that He will work through me. You can do the same as you tackle your day. In the end, all our work—every step of it—belongs to Him.

You can trust God.

ANSWER

TAKE THINGS ONE DAY AT A TIME, AND EVERY MORNING REMEMBER THAT GOD IS IN CONTROL OF IT ALL. YOU CAN TRULY DEPEND ON HIM MINUTE BY MINUTE.

QUESTION 34
WHAT IF I CAN'T DECIDE?

One who isolates himself pursues selfish desires; he rebels against all sound wisdom.—Proverbs 18:1

A quarterback has a lot of decisions to make when it's game time. Although there's a plan in place, he's got to be ready to decide whether to throw the ball, run the ball, or get rid of the ball. It's a lot of pressure, and pressure can make us react in big ways.

When it's time to make a decision, how do you handle it? Do you just go with your gut, that feeling you have inside? Do you ask someone else what they think? Do you search for an answer on Google?

You may not be a quarterback, but you have a lot of decisions and pressure at times. Deciding whether to stick with baseball or golf, choosing which birthday party to go to when they both fall on the same day, and even deciding what to do after school—it can all be hard. But God did not ask you to make decisions by figuring them out alone. God makes Himself and all His wisdom available to you when you read His words in the Bible and when you pray (James 1:5). So ask God for help when making a decision! He will even be with you in the middle of a football game.

You can also learn more about what good decisions look like when reading the Bible. For example, Proverbs is called a book of wisdom because the wisest man who ever lived wrote it (1 Kings 10:23). The book of Job shows us how to handle suffering, and the book of James is about wise living. Every book of the Bible helps us grow in wisdom because "all Scripture is inspired by God and is profitable for teaching, for rebuking, for correcting, for training in righteousness, so that the man of God may be complete, equipped for every good work" (2 Timothy 3:16–17).

You can trust God.

ANSWER

YOU HAVE A GOD WHO WANTS TO HELP YOU MAKE DECISIONS, AND THE ADULTS AROUND YOU WANT TO HELP TOO. ASK FOR WISDOM!

QUESTION 35

WHAT IF I'M TOO YOUNG?

Don't let anyone despise your youth, but set an example for the believers in speech, in conduct, in love, in faith, and in purity.—1 Timothy 4:12

Have you ever wanted to try out for a team, but you weren't old enough yet? Or maybe your neighborhood friends are a little older than you, so they all get to play together, but you're not quite there. It's a disappointing feeling. You want to be part of the game, and maybe even have the skills, but the rules won't allow you to participate yet.

Here's what's cool: You are not too young to have a big impact in God's kingdom.

The Bible teaches us about Timothy who worked in ministry with Paul. Although a lot younger than Paul, Timothy was encouraged that his age did not disqualify him from telling people about Jesus. As today's verse says: "Don't let anyone despise your youth, but set an example for the believers in speech, in conduct, in love, in faith, and in purity."

You are smart. Your thoughts and skills matter. We need you. Younger kids look up to you, but you are admired by a lot of older people too. You don't need a special talent or need to be a specific age to start telling other people about Jesus. Just talk about who He is to you and what He's done!

You are important to the kingdom of God, and He's working through you no matter your age.

You can trust God.

ANSWER

YOUR SIZE AND AGE DO NOT HOLD YOU BACK FROM DOING BIG THINGS FOR GOD. YOU ARE VALUABLE AND GIFTED TO HIM NO MATTER HOW OLD YOU ARE.

QUESTION 36

WHAT IF I CAN'T FALL ASLEEP?

Cast your burden on the LORD, and he will sustain you; he will never allow the righteous to be shaken.—Psalm 55:22

I'm not tired."

How many times have you said that when it's time to go to bed? You lay your head down on your pillow and stare at the ceiling, eyes wide open. Maybe you try counting. Or listening to music. Or playing on your tablet. But none of those things work; you're still not tired. And as the clock ticks, the "what-if" wheel starts to spin. *What if I never fall asleep?* you wonder. *What if I have to do my full day tomorrow on no sleep at all?*

Our minds can easily get way ahead of us—thinking about all that might go wrong—instead of winding down, shutting down, and drifting into sleep.

God will help you when your sleep does not come easily. If you get little rest, God will carry you through the next day, and you'll probably fall asleep more easily the next night! So when you're not tired, choose to focus on God; He's the safest place to direct your thoughts. Pray as you calm your mind. Take some deep breaths to relax your body.

God can give you rest, and He can give you energy on days when you're sleepy. He never needs sleep—that's how powerful He is (Psalm 121:4)!

There's nothing too complicated for Him. Isn't that incredible? So shut out the idea that you're never going to fall asleep. Instead, relax, close your eyes, and give it all to Him.

You can trust God.

ANSWER

FOCUS ON THE MINUTE RIGHT IN FRONT OF YOU AND TRY NOT TO GET WORRIED ABOUT HOURS OF SLEEP (OR NO SLEEP) AHEAD. USE THE TIME TO PRAY, AND SETTLE YOUR MIND BY TALKING TO GOD.

QUESTION 37

WHAT IF NO ONE SEES ME?

"Today salvation has come to this house," Jesus told him, *"because he too is a son of Abraham. For the Son of Man has come to seek and to save the lost."*—Luke 19:9–10

Have you ever looked at a *Where's Waldo?* book? That tiny brown-headed guy in the red and white stripes is always hard to find in a crowd, but it's fun to search through the book and look for him!

Have you ever felt like Waldo? Lost in a crowd? Although finding Waldo is a fun game, when you feel like you're lost in a crowd—unseen and unimportant—it can be a really lonely feeling.

Jesus always has a way of seeing people whom others overlook. Have you ever heard the preschool song about Zacchaeus, the wee, little man? Because he was short, he climbed up in a tree so he could see Jesus over a crowd of people (Luke 19:1–10). When we sing that song, it's easy to get caught up in how short Zacchaeus was and forget the whole point of the story! Jesus picked him out of the crowd and told Zacchaeus He wanted to go to his house.

This wasn't the first or last time Jesus paid special attention to someone in a crowd who was being ignored by everyone else (Mark 5:25–29; 10:46–52). He does not overlook a person He made and He loves, no matter how seemingly insignificant others think that person is. This means Jesus does not overlook you even when others do. What if you viewed yourself the way Jesus did?

More than that, what if you viewed other people the way Jesus did? Do not let your size or age affect how you act. Let people see Jesus through you.

You can trust God.

ANSWER

YOU ARE NEVER OVERLOOKED IN THE EYES OF GOD. YOU MATTER, AND HE SEES YOU!

QUESTION 38

WHAT IF I'M NERVOUS FOR THE FIRST DAY?

"Peace I leave with you. My peace I give to you. I do not give to you as the world gives. Don't let your heart be troubled or fearful."—John 14:27

Do you get the first-day nerves? It might be the first day of school or the first day of a new soccer team. You start thinking about how many days until school starts, where your uniform is, who will be in your class or on your team, what you'll eat for lunch, and where your desk will be.

You're nervous and maybe excited too, and the jitters leave butterflies in your stomach. These "firsts" in life can get you all worked up. Well, there's something you can ask God for every time a "first" moment is approaching: calm.

The God who split the Red Sea in half, walked on water, calmed the storm, and rose from the dead can give you a sense of peace and calm as you head into any nervewracking first day. Ask Him for it! He is powerful and mighty, and He will go with you into your classroom or onto the field.

And remember that Jesus also had "firsts." The Bible says that Jesus became fully man when He left heaven (Philippians 2:7), which means He had to learn and experience everything like you do—for the first time! Jesus can be your peace because He knows what it's like to be human. He walked your road perfectly, and He can help you navigate it.

You can trust God.

ANSWER

GOD WALKS WITH YOU THROUGH EVERY "FIRST." ASK HIM FOR PEACE ABOUT IT ALL.

QUESTION 39

WHAT IF I DON'T WANT TO ASK FOR HELP?

Two are better than one because they have a good reward
for their efforts. For if either falls, his companion can lift him up.
—Ecclesiastes 4:9–10

When you're having a hard time with a math problem or can't figure out your science homework, is it easy for you to ask for help? I hope your answer is yes! If it's not easy, though, let's talk about that for a second, because that was me (and sometimes still is).

Asking for help means having the attention put on me, which I don't like. It also means admitting that I don't understand the assignment or question like everyone else seems to.

The truth is, the longer you stay in your head and worry about what people will think if you ask for help, the longer you delay solving the problem. Your teachers, your friends, your parents . . . they all want to help! And so often, they find joy in helping you figure out things.

God designed us to live our lives with other people, not alone. He knew we'd need each other! That's why after God created Adam, He created Eve.

Genesis 2:18 tells us, "The Lord God said, 'It is not good for the man to be alone. I will make a helper corresponding to him.'"

For every moment you're anxious about asking that question in class, I'd be willing to bet that someone else has the same question. So when you take the step to ask for help, you're giving your friends and classmates permission to do the same. They'll follow your lead!

The people in your life—your parents, siblings, classmates, friends, and teachers—are a gift from God. Be honest. Let them in on what you need, and in return, be the son, brother, classmate, and friend they need as well.

You can trust God.

ANSWER

IT'S OKAY TO ASK FOR HELP! IT DOESN'T MAKE YOU WEAK, AND THE PEOPLE WHO LOVE YOU ARE HAPPY TO DO THEIR PART.

QUESTION 40

WHAT IF I GET IN A FIGHT?

My dear brothers and sisters, understand this: Everyone should be quick to listen, slow to speak, and slow to anger.—James 1:19

Most people love the drama of watching a fight scene in a movie. Crowds form to watch it all go down. You tense up wondering who will win, who will get hurt, and how it will all play out, sometimes imagining how you would react if that were you in the fight. Would you win? Run away? Be the first to throw a punch?

The reality is, a fight isn't exciting when it happens in real life. Whether the fight uses fists or words, it's usually painful and scary. God asks you to work for peace, so how do you keep from physical fights breaking out, and how do you handle fighting words?

Maybe an argument breaks out over something small, like who gets to sit in the best seat in the car. Or the fight might be about something bigger, like a classmate who copies off your paper and then turns in the work as his own.

Thankfully, we don't have to stress over how to deal with conflict and fighting words, because the Bible helps us with that. Today's verse from James 1, for example, tells us three simple steps:

1. Be quick to listen,

2. slow to speak, and

3. slow to anger.

In your most recent argument, did any of these come easily to you? Which one was the hardest? How can you remember to listen first and be slow to anger the next time you're in an argument? All of that is not easy, but did you know that the Holy Spirit, who lives in us as Christians, can help?

When anger and frustration are rising in the room, ask the Holy Spirit to help you stay calm, open your ears to listen, and bite your tongue (figuratively, of course). God knows you can't do this on your own, so He gives you the Holy Spirit to help.

You can trust Him.

ANSWER

NOBODY WANTS TO GET INTO A FIGHT, WHETHER IT'S WITH WORDS OR PHYSICAL, BUT GOD CAN HELP YOU CONTROL YOUR RESPONSE AND FORGIVE WHEN NEEDED.

ACTIVITY DAY

Grab some sticky notes or pieces of paper and tape, and write down some of your favorite Bible verses from the last ten days of devotionals. Which ones have been helpful?

Post the notes around your room or house to help you remember what the Bible says this week. Stick them in places you pass often so that the truth from the Bible "sticks" with you.

You can even add "YCTG" on the bottom of each note as your own special coded reminder that You Can Trust God.

ANSWER RECAP

- When people are mean, choose to be kind. Don't allow hurtful words or actions to define who you are. God defines who you are.

- Use boredom as a chance to get creative. God gave you a beautiful world and smart brain. Use the extra time wisely!

- When there's a lot to get done, take things one day at a time, and every morning remember that God is in control of it all.

- You have a God who wants to help you make decisions, and the adults around you want to help too. Ask for wisdom!

- Your size and age do not hold you back from doing big things for God. You are valuable and gifted to Him no matter how old you are.

- When you can't sleep, use the time to pray. Settle your mind by talking to God.

- You are never overlooked by God. You matter, and He sees you!

- God walks with you through every "first." Ask Him for peace about it all.

- It's okay to ask for help! It doesn't make you weak, and the people who love you are happy to do their part.

- God can help you control your response in a fight and forgive when needed.

QUESTION 41

WHAT IF THEY'RE BETTER THAN ME?

"I know the plans I have for you"—this is the Lord's declaration—
"plans for your well-being, not for disaster, to give you a future
and a hope."—Jeremiah 29:11

In middle school, my gym teacher taught us how to shoot a bow and arrow. I was so bad at it! Every time I pulled the bowstring back, the arrow would hit the ground, but I kept noticing my classmates were hitting the target and making it look easy. The more I tried, the more frustrated I got.

Can you relate? Has there ever been a sport or a subject at school that's felt hard for you but seemed easy for others?

It's easy to compare yourself to your friends or teammates. You can get caught up in competing for good grades, performing as well, or attracting the kind of attention they do.

But God has a plan that's just for you. It's not the exact same plan as the one He has for your brother or your sister. It's as unique as you are.

God has given you a distinct personality and your own special set of talents; He created you to be your own person. So be happy for your friends, your siblings, and your classmates. Encourage them. Be supportive. Then walk confidently as the person God created you to be.

Let go of the worry that you won't be able to do everything as well as everyone else, because the world doesn't need you to be them. The world needs you to be you! It needs your smart, kind, talented self. God made you in His image, which means you are the exact reflection of Him that He wanted to make. And that's enough.

And when you see others hitting every target, cheer them on! God is delighted when you do.

You can trust God.

ANSWER

THERE'S ALWAYS GOING TO BE SOMEONE WHO'S BETTER AT SOMETHING THAN YOU ARE, BECAUSE GOD GAVE US EACH UNIQUE TALENTS. IT'S SOMETHING TO CELEBRATE INSTEAD OF ENVY!

QUESTION 42

WHAT IF I DON'T HAVE WHAT I NEED?

My God will supply all your needs according to his riches in glory in Christ Jesus.—Philippians 4:19

Have you ever walked to the counter to pay for something and realized you were short a few dollars? Maybe you saved the cash from your birthday card and added it to the cash you got for mowing your neighbor's yard. You walked into the store dead set on getting the game you've been wishing for, but you quickly realized you didn't have what you needed to buy it.

Those moments are disappointing and frustrating! Sometimes not having what you need is bigger than being short a few dollars. Maybe your family is struggling with money right now, so you're not sure if you'll have enough money in your school account to buy lunch or be able to go on the class field trip. Maybe you're not feeling well, and you don't know if you have the right kind of medicine at home to help. It can all cause a lot of worry.

Can I tell you that God hasn't forgotten about you in those moments? He can show up over and over again and provide exactly what you need.

In the book of Exodus, the Bible tells us that the Israelites wandered in the desert for decades, waiting to be taken to the land God had promised them.

Can you imagine how many times they asked, "Are we there yet?" Day after day, God provided exactly what the Israelites needed to help them get through. He literally made it rain bread for them (Exodus 16:4)!

And God will give you what you need too. You can ask Him for help with money, for healing, or for patience and courage through it all. Some days you may need something physical—for a stomachache to go away or your eyes to quit itching from allergies. Other days you may need something for your heart—a joyful reminder or help calming your nerves. God can show up with exactly what you need.

Sometimes He even shows up with something unexpected—something we didn't know we needed! God will provide one way or another. He is good.

You can trust God.

ANSWER

PSALM 23:1 SAYS, "THE Lord IS MY SHEPHERD; I HAVE WHAT I NEED." HE WILL TAKE CARE OF YOU!

QUESTION 43

WHAT IF I'M TRYING TO STAY OUT OF TROUBLE?

Do not be conformed to this age, but be transformed by the renewing of your mind, so that you may discern what is the good, pleasing, and perfect will of God.—Romans 12:2

When we were growing up, my oldest brother convinced my other brother to jump from our tree house in the backyard. Bad idea? Probably. Did my brother get pressured into doing it? Yep. One broken arm and many years later, he still hasn't forgotten that story.

How easily are other people able to persuade you to do something you know you shouldn't do? Peer pressure is tricky, and it can keep your mind spinning. You want to stand up for yourself and what you believe. But you also don't want to miss out on everything your friends are doing!

Sometimes it can feel like you're choosing between what your parents and other adults want for you (safety) and what your friends or other peers want you to do (adventure). In every situation, you have to decide what is wise. Remember, you and your friends will experience tons of safe yet adventurous moments. Others might seem fun at first but are actually dangerous or even disobedient.

So, how do you know what's wise and what's trouble?

The Bible tells us to choose God's way over the world's way, and we can figure out God's way by staying close to Him. God also gave us the Holy Spirit, His Helper, to nudge us when we're getting off track and making bad decisions. Trust Him.

In the book of Genesis, God said that Adam and Eve could eat fruit from any of the gorgeous trees in the garden of Eden except for one. Did they listen? Nope. They chose trouble, and there were life-changing consequences. God was very clear with His instructions, and He's very clear with you as well. You don't have to guess what's right and wrong because He's laid it out for you in the Bible.

You can trust God.

ANSWER

THE BIBLE IS YOUR GUIDE TO WHAT'S RIGHT AND WRONG. IT'S YOUR MOST HELPFUL RESOURCE FOR MAKING GOOD DECISIONS!

QUESTION 44

WHAT IF I CAN'T WAIT?

Rejoice in hope; be patient in affliction; be persistent in prayer.
—Romans 12:12

Sometimes you live in a series of "can't waits." You can't wait until summer camp. You can't wait until Christmas. You can't wait until you're old enough to have a cell phone. You can't wait until school is out. You can't wait to drive.

Whatever the thing may be, the anticipation for it can feel more emotional than the actual moment you are waiting on! It's fun to be excited about something that's still to come, but does your "can't wait" feeling sometimes give you a negative attitude? Do you ever end up grumpy, impatient, or frustrated? "This is taking forever!" "Why aren't we there yet?!"

As you wait for exciting things, "rejoice in hope" as Romans 12:12 says. Remember that every good gift comes from "the Father of lights" (James 1:17) and that His timing is better than ours. Be content with where you are *now*. Take any impatience to Jesus in prayer.

Do you know what I can't wait for? I can't wait for the day Jesus returns! On that day He will restore the earth to what it once was, and we will live in peace forever with Him. This will be the most exciting thing ever! But the days of waiting for that day are long. Sometimes I let the positive feeling of waiting for Jesus give way to my negative thoughts. Sometimes I get too focused on myself and forget to rejoice in hope and choose joy.

The day will come when you no longer have to wait for good things and all you will know is joy. But guess what? Jesus isn't hiding from you until that day. He's with you, even now, as you wait.

You can trust God.

ANSWER

ASK GOD FOR PATIENCE WHEN WAITING FEELS HARD, BUT ALSO ASK HIM TO TEACH YOU SOMETHING WHILE YOU WAIT.

QUESTION 45

WHAT IF GOD CAN'T HEAR ME?

Draw near to God, and he will draw near to you.—James 4:8

Have you ever been on a video chat when your internet starts going out? Suddenly your face is frozen on the screen or your words sound choppy, and your friends or classmates are staring at you confused.

"Can you hear me?"

You're practically yelling at the screen, yet everyone on the other side can't hear a thing.

Sometimes it seems like the same thing when you're talking to God. Maybe He hasn't answered a prayer request you've made for years, or perhaps you feel like one bad thing is happening after another in your life. You're left wondering if you and God have a good connection. "Hello, God? Am I muted?" you ask.

The Bible tells us that if we come near to God, He'll come near to us. Now, that may seem confusing, because we can't physically see God. So how do we come near to Him? Imagine He's sitting there next to you. Pray. Talk to Him and tell Him why you're thankful for Him. Ask Him for what you need. Trust that He hears every word (because He does!).

You don't have to rely on a Wi-Fi connection or phone to know God or pray! He always hears you. God may not answer your prayer the way you thought He would, but He always has a bigger plan in mind. If He's not sharing that plan with you, open your Bible. Read about His promises, and hear what He said to His people about His plans for them.

If you feel like you can't hear God, remember that you have an entire Bible full of His words. Read them. Pray them. God will be close, and He will hear it all.

You can trust Him.

ANSWER

EVEN WHEN YOU FEEL LIKE GOD'S REALLY FAR AWAY, HE'S NOT. HE CAN HEAR YOU, AND HE LOVES YOU.

QUESTION 46

WHAT IF MY STOMACH HURTS BECAUSE I'M NERVOUS?

I am certain that I will see the LORD's goodness in the land of the living. Wait for the LORD; be strong, and let your heart be courageous. Wait for the LORD.—Psalm 27:13–14

Today's reading is not about bathroom jokes, but I know you'd love it if it was.

Some days, the craziness of what's going on around you will be too much, and it will start to affect your body. Sometimes your nerves will work so hard that you get a stomachache. It's okay if this happens! It's actually very normal.

Anxiety isn't a new issue. Even in the Bible we see people like King David experiencing deep worry and fear. He says in Psalm 139:23 (NIV), "Search me, God, and know my heart; test me and know my anxious thoughts."

Physical pain is sometimes a reminder of what's actually going on in our minds and hearts. You can take some medicine to help a stomach or headache, but what can you do to calm your nerves and hopefully prevent the aching?

Tell God what you're nervous about! He wants to hear from you, and today's verse reminds you that you can be courageous while you wait on God. He's strong, and you can be too. Tell someone around you what you're nervous about too. Sometimes saying it out loud takes away some of the fear. Plus, I bet your friends and family have some helpful advice or tips to offer.

Don't be embarrassed in these moments when you feel off because the nerves have taken over. You're not weak. You're human.

You can trust God.

Answer

Our bodies do crazy things, but you can talk to God about your nerves, your stomach, and what you're scared about. Nothing is too small for Him.

QUESTION 47

WHAT IF I DON'T WANT TO CRY?

He comforts us in all our affliction, so that we may be able to comfort those who are in any kind of affliction, through the comfort we ourselves receive from God.—2 Corinthians 1:4

I hate the feeling of holding back tears. My throat feels like I'm swallowing rocks, my eyes fill up, and sometimes my cheeks turn red. I often hold back tears because I don't want anyone else to see me cry. I don't want the attention or have to talk about why the tears are there.

How do you feel about crying?

A lot of times, adults can be hard on boys about crying because we talk so much about how strong you are. It's true! You are strong. And so are girls. But you are all totally allowed to cry and show your emotions.

Think about Jesus. The Bible tells us He felt a lot of pain and sorrow (Isaiah 53:3). While He was on earth, He cried (John 11:35). He knew sadness, and your hurt isn't a mystery to Him. Jesus knows what your sadness is, and He knows what sadness feels like.

You can also let someone else know you're sad. They may not be able to fix everything, but they can help you not feel so alone when your heart hurts.

Sometimes the greatest gift is just having someone else to sit with you or listen.

Being sad is not a weakness; otherwise, Jesus would have been weak! Sadness is just an emotion you feel from time to time, and that's okay. Sadness reminds you that this world is not what it should be; it reminds you that you need God. You have a God who both comforts and heals. Lean on Him in your sadness because He can carry you. His power is greater than your tears.

You can trust Him.

ANSWER

GOD IS NOT AFRAID OF YOUR TEARS. IT'S OKAY TO BE SAD OR MAD AND LET THE TEARS FALL. IT DOES NOT MAKE YOU WEAK.

QUESTION 48

WHAT IF THINGS DON'T GET BETTER?

May the God of hope fill you with all joy and peace as you believe so that you may overflow with hope by the power of the Holy Spirit.—Romans 15:13

Have you ever jumped into a giant foam pit? Every time you make a move to get out, you start sinking back in, and it almost feels easier just to lay there and let it take over than it does to fight to get out.

I know your life can sometimes have so many things going on that you feel like you're sinking too. One day you get a bad grade, the next day your mom has a scary diagnosis at the doctor, and the next day your team loses the tournament. It's hard to find the good in anything when all you feel is bad. I've been there.

Today, we're looking at Romans 15:13. The book of Romans was written by Paul, who definitely knew what it was like to have one thing after the other go wrong. Paul spent a lot of his ministry locked up in jail because people weren't happy that he was talking about Jesus. Do you know what he did while he was in jail, though? He kept praying, he kept worshiping God, and he kept talking about Jesus. He knew where true hope comes from. It comes from God, not from our circumstances.

We can't know if one bad thing might come after another, but we can change the way we think about the bad things. Just as Paul chose to have hope on the hard days, we can too! And this isn't an empty, take-a-chance kind of hope. We have hope because we've watched God fulfill every promise He's ever made in the Bible and we know that in the end, He wins! Our hope is not about bad things stopping now. It's about Jesus getting rid of the bad things forever, when He decides to.

Until that day comes, you still have God here with you. When you become a Christian, the Holy Spirit comes to live in you and can give you the peace and hope you need to get through each day—whatever it brings.

You can trust God.

ANSWER

THERE IS HOPE. GOD IS ALWAYS WITH YOU, AND YOUR BAD DAYS AREN'T A MYSTERY TO HIM. HE CARES.

QUESTION 49

WHAT IF I'M SCARED OF A DISASTER?

"Haven't I commanded you: be strong and courageous? Do not be afraid or discouraged, for the LORD your God is with you wherever you go."—Joshua 1:9

Have you ever hoped a fire drill or tornado drill would happen right before your math test so you wouldn't have to take it? Maybe that's just me! I would accept any interruption necessary to get out of taking a test.

These days you have to practice a lot of school drills. Although it might mean getting out of class for a few minutes, your stomach might do a few turns when you imagine a fire actually burning down the building!

We practice these drills for the same reason we practice our multiplication tables and spelling. We do them so when we need them, our response comes naturally. We know exactly what to do and how to do it.

It all can be a little bit scary though. So many "What-if?" questions can leave you feeling unsafe. So here's what I want you to do: Just as you would prepare for an earthquake by having a drill, you can also prepare for scary moments by memorizing verses from the Bible. Look for verses related to fear, and think about the words.

When you memorize what the Bible says, you can rely on God's truth when you're afraid. You can say in your head:

- God is with me wherever I go (Joshua 1:9).

- God will strengthen me and help me (Isaiah 41:10).

- God is coming to my rescue (Isaiah 35:4).

You cannot prevent fires, tornadoes, earthquakes, or other disasters. These things are out of your hands. What you can do is trust that God is always with you, and if disasters come, He will help you through.

You can trust God.

ANSWER

NOTHING IS A SURPRISE TO GOD. HE WILL BE YOUR STRENGTH IF SOMETHING SCARY HAPPENS. WHEN YOU'RE FEELING WORRIED, REPEAT VERSES FROM GOD'S WORD TO YOURSELF.

QUESTION 50

WHAT IF I GET OVERWHELMED?

After these events, the word of the Lord came to Abram in a vision: "Do not be afraid, Abram. I am your shield; your reward will be very great."—Genesis 15:1

When you have a ton of homework, football practice after school, and lines to memorize for the play, how does it make you feel? Maybe you're struggling to understand something new in your science class and you're scared about the big test coming up. Maybe you don't know how to do the new move your coach just taught you. Or maybe your part in the play isn't the one you wanted.

Does having loads to do make you want to give up? Do you feel like you don't even want to try?

When you get overwhelmed, it can make you feel like anything and everything is too much. Your mom may ask you to clean your room, and you snap back at her that you can't. Your friend may ask you to help with something after school, and you ignore him because the very thought of doing one more thing is too much. Everything keeps coming at you.

I love what today's verse says about God being your shield. Can you picture that? You're standing in a battle, and as things are flying at you, trying to knock you down, God is the shield. He's the barrier protecting you and helping you to stay standing.

It may not look like it all the time, but we are all in a battle every day. Things are being thrown at us from all directions, and God is the shield. So when you're overwhelmed, don't sit down in the middle of the battle. Don't turn your back and walk away. Most importantly, don't lay down the shield, forgetting about God. Trust that He will help you keep fighting, no matter what comes your way.

You can trust God.

ANSWER

GOD WILL FIGHT FOR YOU AND PROVIDE FOR YOU. HE CAN GIVE YOU THE STRENGTH AND ENERGY YOU NEED TO KEEP GOING.

ACTIVITY DAY

Grab a piece of paper and something to draw with, and draw a big circle or a big cloud. In it, list out (or draw) things that are worrying you this week.

Then, using a different color, next to each thing worrying you, write out something you have learned about God that is helping you.

Use this picture as a reminder that God is with you no matter what you're worried about!

ANSWER RECAP

- If someone is better than you at something, remember that God gave us each unique talents. It's something to celebrate!

- Psalm 23:1 says, "The Lord is my shepherd; I have what I need." He will take care of you!

- The Bible is your guide to what's right and wrong. It's your most helpful resource for making good decisions!

- Ask God for patience when waiting feels hard, but also ask Him to teach you something while you wait.

- Even when you feel like God's really far away, He's not. He can hear you, and He loves you.

- When you're nervous, you can talk to God about your nerves and your fears. Nothing is too small for Him.

- God is not afraid of your tears. It's okay to be sad or mad and let the tears fall. It does not make you weak.

- There is hope. God is always with you, and your bad days aren't a mystery to Him. He cares.

- If you're scared of a disaster, remember that nothing is a surprise to God. He will be your strength if something scary happens.

- When you're overwhelmed, God will provide for you. He can give you strength and energy to keep going.

QUESTION 51

WHAT IF I HATE TESTS?

I lift my eyes toward the mountains. Where will my help come from?
My help comes from the LORD, the Maker of heaven and earth.
—Psalm 121:1–2

When I was a kid, taking tests always made me nervous, especially standardized tests. The prep work, the pressure, the long instructions—test day always felt intimidating! When the classroom got quiet and the teacher finished reading out instructions, I was left with letters swirling on a page, multiple-choice answer bubbles to fill in, and a racing heart. Could I pass the test?

Some test days aren't as intense as that, but there's often something coming that you have to prepare for—a spelling test, memorizing multiplication tables, or studying the capitals of each state. Although you might have someone to study with, when test day arrives, it's all in your hands (or should I say in your brain?).

Taking tests can feel like standing at the start of an obstacle course. You know it's going to be a challenge, and you think you know how to complete the job, but there's a lot of hops, skips, and jumps ahead of you (and some fear can easily creep in). Plus, getting past the obstacles is all up to you, which can feel really overwhelming.

Take a look at today's verse. Even though growing up means doing more and more things on your own (which is exciting!), you never truly have to get by on your own. God is with you. When you're taking a hard test or tackling an obstacle course, ask God to calm your mind so you can recall the things you studied. Also ask Him to remind you that a test is just a test; it's not your life. Ask Him to give you steady breathing and the right perspective so that you can give it your best.

Rely on God for help. You will realize quickly that big responsibilities are less scary when you believe you are not alone.

You can trust God.

ANSWER

IF YOU'RE NERVOUS OR UNPREPARED FOR A TEST, YOU CAN TELL GOD. HE CAN HELP YOU CALM DOWN AND MAKE IT THROUGH. IT'S NOT TOO SMALL OF A DETAIL FOR HIM.

Question 52

What If I Can't Keep Up?

Therefore encourage one another and build each other up as you are already doing.—1 Thessalonians 5:11

I ran out on the volleyball court determined that my serve would be great this time. It would wow everyone. It was going to make it over the net without hitting anything (including a person). But my hopes and dreams died a little because that volleyball went flying the wrong way and landed far outside the lines, making it a bad serve. I just couldn't keep up with how good some of my classmates were at volleyball.

It's not a fun feeling when you can't do what someone else can. Sometimes it's because you're just not quite old enough, sometimes you don't have that skill, and sometimes it's just not your turn. Whatever the case, I'm going to challenge you to be an encourager to those around you instead of focusing on what you can't do.

Pat your buddy on the back when he does a good job. Go up to the guy who always outruns you and tell him one good thing you see in him. You'll be surprised at how people respond to your kindness, and your attitude will begin to shift.

Not being able to keep up doesn't make you weak; it makes you human. You're not going to be good at everything, so how can you cheer on the good (and the gifts) you see in others? As you encourage other people, they might catch on and start to encourage you too. God's not playing favorites when He gives different people different gifts.

God knows what He's doing.

You can trust God.

ANSWER

GOD IS MORE CONCERNED WITH YOUR HEART THAN YOUR PERFORMANCE. DON'T FOCUS ON KEEPING UP OR BEING THE BEST. BE GRATEFUL FOR THE ABILITIES GOD HAS CHOSEN JUST FOR YOU!

Question 53

What If I'm Not Sure What's True?

The entirety of your word is truth, each of your righteous judgments endures forever.—Psalm 119:160

How many times have you read an advertisement and wondered, "Is that true?" It's like in the movie *Elf* when Buddy sees the sign for "World's Best Coffee!" and goes inside the diner to congratulate everyone. The sign might make you want to try the coffee, but is it *really* the world's best? How do we know?

There's so much information being thrown at you—from school, from friends, from home, from the internet. When you're trying to figure out what's true and what's a lie, ask questions!

Even if you're nervous, don't be afraid to ask. Open your Bible and see what God says. And talk to a parent or teacher to help you find and understand the truth.

Unfortunately, the devil would prefer to confuse you and keep you distracted. It's his favorite game because when you're confused, you easily take your eyes off Jesus and start believing things that aren't true.

But God is not a God of confusion (1 Corinthians 14:33). He's clear, and He's given us instructions to live by in the Bible. Ask Him to help you figure out what's true. Read your Bible and memorize verses so you can compare the truth of what it says to things you hear.

You have what you need because God has given you Himself, His Word, and people to help you find out what's true.

You can trust God.

ANSWER

DON'T BE AFRAID TO ASK QUESTIONS. GOD IS NOT A GOD OF CONFUSION, SO TRUST THAT WHAT THE BIBLE (GOD'S WORD) SAYS IS TRUE. HE IS NOT GOING TO LEAD YOU IN THE WRONG DIRECTION.

Question 54

What If Following the Rules Is Hard?

He is our God, and we are the people of his pasture, the sheep under his care.—Psalm 95:7

One of the hardest rules to follow as a kid is not running at the pool. It's like asking you to take all your excitement and remove it from your body. You'd much rather get a running start before a cannonball jump, and you of course want to beat your friend into the pool so you can catch the football. Don't run? Tough.

But I've seen what slipping and falling by the pool can do, and it usually equals a trip to the emergency room. The rule exists because the consequences can really cause some damage.

Does it ever feel like you're surrounded by too many rules? You have rules on the school bus, rules in art class, rules on the field, and rules at home. Does following the rules come easily to you, or is it a challenge?

The Bible often compares humans to sheep. I hate to break it you, but sheep aren't known for being super smart. That's why they need a shepherd watching over them and a fence to keep them contained. Without those things, the sheep wander, get lost, and risk being hurt or attacked by another animal.

Rules and boundaries keep us humans contained and protected too. It might feel like the rules are only keeping us from having fun—but the truth is, they prevent us from getting hurt.

When the rules are hard to follow, trust that your parents, teachers, coaches, and God have put rules in place to help you grow and keep you safe. Your Shepherd, God, especially has your best interests in mind. He knows exactly what you need.

You can trust God.

ANSWER

REMEMBER THAT GOD'S RULES WERE CREATED OUT OF LOVE AND PROTECTION. THEY EXIST TO HELP YOU LIVE A LIFE HE DESIGNED FOR YOUR GOOD, NOT TO HOLD YOU BACK.

QUESTION 55
WHAT IF I KEEP MESSING UP?

He said to me, "My grace is sufficient for you, for my power is perfected in weakness."—2 Corinthians 12:9

Have you ever found yourself getting in trouble at home or grounded over and over again? It's almost like driving bumper cars and ending up wedged into a corner, just bumping into the same things over and over again, looking for a way out.

When you get stuck in this place of getting into trouble or messing up all the time, it can really make you feel down and even sad and angry. You want to do better, but it's hard! Here are some steps you can take.

First, as soon as you realize you've done something wrong, name what it is and agree with God that it is sin. Then ask Him to forgive you. Pray for forgiveness, and then go to the person you've hurt (or disobeyed) and ask for forgiveness. Second, figure out a plan to help you resist the temptation to do the same thing again. Ask an adult to figure this out with you!

God has given you grace, a gift you do not deserve. Grace is like jumping into a deep swimming pool and feeling the weight go away as you float back to the top. Through God's grace, He takes your guilt and shame and carries it for you so you can swim through life without that sinking feeling about your sin. And God will never quit doing that for you. He will never stop showing you grace.

That may seem like a crazy idea—that He would never give up on you—but God's grace never runs out.

Even if you keep messing up, you can trust God.

ANSWER

GOD ISN'T GOING TO WALK AWAY FROM YOU. HE WILL CONTINUE TO HELP YOU DO BETTER AND FORGIVE YOU WHEN YOU GET IT WRONG. HE'S A SAFE PLACE TO GO EVERY TIME YOU MESS UP.

QUESTION 56

WHAT IF THE NEWS IS SCARY?

Do not be conquered by evil, but conquer evil with good.
—Romans 12:21

Do you often listen to the news? Where do you get your news from? Do your parents talk about the news a lot, or do they tend to avoid it? The news keeps us informed about what's going on in our city, our country, and the world, but sometimes it's scary to hear. Although there's plenty of good news to share, our attention usually goes to the unsettling stories that leave us wondering, *What if that happens to me?*

It's okay to turn off the news.

If the stories are too hard to watch, you don't have to watch them. We want to be aware of what's going on around us while not being shut down by it all. The truth is, our world is a broken place, and unfortunately, there is always going to be bad news. Jesus said, "You will have suffering in this world." But in the very next sentence, He said, "Be courageous! I have conquered the world" (John 16:33). Because we know Jesus, we will *always* have good news.

The next time you are scared because of something you see on the news, do two things: First, pray and ask God for peace and believe that He's with you. Also pray that God would help the people who are part of the story.

Second, consider what you can do to bring good news (Jesus!) to people around you. Can you make a card for someone to encourage them? Can you take some flowers to the neighbors to brighten their day? Can you tell your friends how much Jesus loves them?

The world is a dark place, but Jesus is the Light (John 1:5). You get to be a light in a dark world, because Jesus is the Light in you. Scary news cannot put out that light.

You can trust God.

ANSWER

GOD KNEW THE WORLD WOULD HOLD SOME SCARY NEWS, BUT HE ALSO GAVE US THE GREATEST NEWS EVER: WE CAN HAVE ETERNAL LIFE WITH HIM.

QUESTION 57

WHAT IF I DON'T KNOW WHEN TO PRAY?

I want the men in every place to pray, lifting up holy hands without anger or argument.—1 Timothy 2:8

Have you tried telling adults a story or asking a question, and they say, "I can't talk right now"? It can be frustrating, especially if you have something urgent to say.

Maybe you think God is the same way, and you wonder when is the right time to talk to Him. At church? Before a meal? At bedtime? Actually, you can and should talk to Him anytime you want to! He's never too busy, and He can always be interrupted.

Sometimes you might forget that talking to God first is the best option. It's natural to have a bad day and immediately turn to a friend or family member about your frustrations, but the God who created you wants you to come to Him. He knows what you're going through and can carry it for you.

And, unlike the people in our lives, God is always available to listen. When I decide to talk to Him about what's bothering me, it never fails: as soon as I start praying, the anger or other emotions start to settle. This doesn't mean the issue is immediately resolved, but He always gives an invitation to calm down, no matter where or when.

What's bothering you this week? What are you excited about or worried about? Have you told God? He's bigger and better than any other listener because He knows what's on your mind completely. He knows what you've been through and what's still to come. So the next time you have something to talk about, pray to God first and talk to people second. It will change everything.

You can trust God.

ANSWER

TALK TO GOD LIKE YOU WOULD TALK TO A FRIEND, WHENEVER AND WHEREVER. HE CREATED YOU, HE LOVES YOU, AND HE IS ALWAYS LISTENING.

QUESTION 58

WHAT IF I DON'T HAVE ALL THE INFORMATION?

Now faith is the reality of what is hoped for, the proof of what is not seen.—Hebrews 11:1

Have you ever gone on a walk, hike, or run and realized pretty quickly you didn't know what you were getting yourself into? Maybe you thought it was an easy walk, but the weather was hotter than you realized, so you're soon dripping with sweat. Or the hiking trail was steeper and longer than you thought, so you're thirsty and tired with no idea how much longer it's going to take to get to the end. Or you showed up for gym class and realized you were running today, but you wore the shoes that give you blisters.

When you don't have all the information before you start something, does it make you worried? Do you need to know what to bring, what to wear, what you're going to do, and how long it will last before you feel okay to go?

There's nothing wrong with wanting to know what to expect, and having all the details is helpful! But life requires faith and flexibility too. The Bible defines faith as "the reality of what is hoped for, the proof of what is not seen" (Hebrews 11:1). In many ways, *faith* is another word for trust. When you end up in a situation you didn't plan for and the changes make you nervous, you can have faith that God will help you through it.

Hebrews 11 is often referred to as "The Hall of Faith" chapter, which I love. It talks about the faithful acts of Noah, Abraham, Sarah, Isaac, Moses, and more. (Go check it out!) None of these people had all the information or knew what God's plan was, but they each acted on faith. They trusted that God knew what He was doing. And you know what? They realized His plan was always better (Hebrews 11:40).

You can trust God.

ANSWER

CHOOSE TO TRUST THAT GOD WILL HELP YOU THROUGH WHEN YOU DON'T FEEL PREPARED. "FAITH AND FLEXIBILITY" MIGHT BE YOUR NEW MOTTO FOR THE DAY!

QUESTION 59

WHAT IF I'M WORRIED ABOUT TOMORROW?

"Don't worry about tomorrow, because tomorrow will worry about itself. Each day has enough trouble of its own."—Matthew 6:34

If any of your relatives are doctors, then here's my apology to them now. I hate going to the doctor. I put off making appointments because I don't want to go, even though I know it's good to keep my body healthy. Once the appointment is confirmed, I dread the day as it gets closer. The night before I'm typically a little nervous, a little mad, and a little worried. Do you ever feel that way?

Worrying about what's coming tomorrow can send your mind on a fast train down tracks that may not exist. You can start creating ideas of how tomorrow will go and be completely off the rails about it. Sometimes you spend so much effort thinking about what might or might not happen that you miss the good happening right now in front of you.

In the book of Matthew, Jesus reminds us not to be anxious. He says, "Consider the birds of the sky: They don't sow or reap or gather into barns, yet your heavenly Father feeds them. Aren't you worth more than they?" (6:26).

Your worry can often translate into a need to control what happens tomorrow. You might worry about your upcoming game, your to-do list, or if your friends will still like you. But can you imagine the birds doing that? God created the birds and everything they need—and He created you too.

Do you think God is worried about what will happen tomorrow? (Hint: He's not.)

As you start your day, think about God's creation around you. The trees aren't worried about blossoming tomorrow. The grass isn't worried about growing tomorrow. The sun isn't worried about rising tomorrow. God's creation continues to work to the sound of His voice, and He will care for you both today *and* tomorrow.

You can trust God.

ANSWER

FOCUS ON THE GOOD HAPPENING TODAY, AND REMEMBER THAT GOD HAS ALREADY TAKEN CARE OF TOMORROW.

Question 60

What If I Oversleep?

"May the Lord make his face shine on you and be gracious to you."
—Numbers 6:25

When my brother was a teenager, it was impossible to get him out of bed in the mornings. Thankfully, that wasn't my job, but I remember him always sleeping through his alarm, and my parents were always having to go in his room multiple times to try to wake him. I think they finally gave up and decided if he was late and had detention for the rest of high school, that was his problem!

Do you ever oversleep or worry that you will?

Here's the thing: stuff like this will happen every now and then. Even when you plan ahead and check your alarm twice, or you remind your parents you need to be up earlier than normal, something will go wrong and you'll oversleep. But you know what? It's okay! One chaotic morning won't ruin your entire life; it doesn't mean it will happen every day; and it certainly doesn't mean God has run out of grace for you.

When you're planning for the next day, do the things you can control: set the alarm, check in with your parents, and then trust God with it. If something goes wrong the next morning, take a deep breath and pray. Ask God for a reset moment, and trust that He will provide it. Just as the sun rises every single morning, you can have a fresh start (even when your first start feels stressful). The Bible tells us God's mercies are new every morning (Lamentations 3:22–23). And guess what? That's true whether you wake up on time or not!

You can trust God.

Answer

Take a deep breath. God still has control of the time and control of your day.

ACTIVITY DAY

It's helpful to learn how to pray to God about anything and everything. You can practice this by writing a letter to God. Let Him know what's going on in your life and how you're feeling. Tell Him what's worrying you. Ask Him to help! Let Him know what you're learning about Him. Let this exercise remind you that you can take anything to Him.

ANSWER RECAP

- If you're nervous or unprepared for a test, you can tell God. He can help you calm down and make it through.

- God is more concerned with your heart than your performance. Don't focus on keeping up or being the best.

- Don't be afraid to ask questions. God is not a God of confusion, so trust that what the Bible (God's Word) says is true.

- Remember that God's rules were created out of love and protection. They exist to help you live a life He designed for your good.

- God isn't going to walk away when you mess up. He will continue to help you do better and forgive you when you get it wrong.

- God knew the world would hold some scary news, but He also gave us the greatest news ever: we can have eternal life with Him.

- Talk to God like you would talk to a friend, whenever and wherever. He created you, He loves you, and He is always listening.

- Choose to trust that God will help you through when you don't feel prepared. "Faith and Flexibility" might be your new motto!

- Focus on the good happening today, and remember that God has already taken care of tomorrow.

- Take a deep breath. God still has control of the time and control of your day.

QUESTION 61

WHAT IF I'M DIFFERENT THAN MY FAMILY?

The Spirit himself testifies together with our spirit that we are God's children, and if children, also heirs—heirs of God and coheirs with Christ.—Romans 8:16–17

Let me go ahead and answer today's question. If you're different from your family . . . good! Your family needs your unique self. God created each of us with our own personalities, looks, style, and interests. It's super common that siblings and parents share some of those things, but being different doesn't make you an outcast in your family. It makes you special.

Maybe your whole family is into baseball, but you would rather be skateboarding. Or maybe everyone at your house loves to crank up the music, but you'd rather be in your room with a book. You might be different in those ways, but you're still an important part of the family.

And if the word *family* feels a bit icky because your family feels broken or out of reach, here are some reminders from the Bible about the family of God you belong to (and your Father God, who can be trusted).

- You have been adopted by God and given a new identity in Him (John 1:12).

- You have a Father who not only loves you—He's delighted about you (Zephaniah 3:17).

- You have brothers and sisters because other followers of Jesus are your brothers and sisters in Jesus (Romans 12:5).

- You are a son of the King (2 Corinthians 6:18).

- ou are not forgotten or left out. You are not an afterthought or a plan B. You are chosen and cherished by God (Isaiah 43:1).

- You have a forever family because you will spend forever with God and with your brothers and sisters in Christ (Romans 8:29–30).

God is so creative that He was able to make each of us unique. And we each have a place in His diverse and beautiful family.

You are always welcome, and you can trust God.

ANSWER

BEING DIFFERENT IS NOT A BAD THING, BUT YOU BELONG NO MATTER WHAT. YOU ARE LOVED FOR WHO YOU ARE, AND YOU BELONG TO GOD.

QUESTION 62

WHAT IF MY PARENTS' JOBS CHANGE?

I sought the LORD, and he answered me and rescued me from all my fears.—Psalm 34:4

What do you imagine doing for your job when you get older? Do you want to be an engineer or a teacher? A musician or a veterinarian? A computer programmer or a plumber? It is so fun to think about the future and even start practicing now!

What do your parents or guardians do for work? Is it a job you know a lot about? Do they travel often? Work from home? Go to an office every day?

Adults' jobs come and go, and they can change quickly. This is totally normal, but it can be scary for kids when you don't know how it will affect you. You wonder, *Will we have to move? Will my parent(s) be unhappy? What if we don't have enough money until the next job?*

Job changes can bring up a lot of questions and emotions. Thankfully, your parents' jobs aren't something you need to control. Although their work affects you, it's one more thing you can trust God to handle. So when you hear conversations about new jobs, lost jobs, stressful jobs, or jobs in other towns, don't let that scare you.

God has a plan for your parents' or guardians' lives, just as He has a plan for yours. He cares about their jobs and the work they do. He can be trusted with the jobs they have, the jobs they want, and the jobs they gain or lose. And one day, when you fill out your first job application, you can rely on God to take care of your job too!

You can trust God.

ANSWER

GOD ALWAYS HAS A PLAN, SO YOU DON'T HAVE TO WORRY ABOUT FIGURING OUT EVERY DETAIL OF WHAT'S NEXT. TRUST THAT HE'S GOING TO TAKE CARE OF YOUR PARENTS AND YOUR FAMILY.

QUESTION 63
WHAT IF I CAN'T GET ALL A'S?

Whatever you do, in word or in deed, do everything in the name of the Lord Jesus, giving thanks to God the Father through him.
—Colossians 3:17

How important are grades to you? When I was younger, I remember waiting for report cards to be passed out (yes, that's before all the grades were posted online). I would get really upset if I saw anything lower than an "A" on the report card because I was slightly too concerned about being a good student.

Do report-card days make you nervous? Sometimes it's exciting to see your grades, and sometimes you dread it. It all depends on what the report card says! Whatever the case, how much time do you spend thinking about those grades? Most of us want to do well in class. But sometimes a subject in school is just plain tough, and the A's are hard to come by.

Here's the good news: God's not worried about the letters on your report card. He's more concerned about your heart and mind.

Does this mean you don't have to study or do your schoolwork? Nope! It's always a good idea to try your best. But as you think about grades, look at today's verse.

God gave you a quick mind. Using that gift for His glory is what matters most. That means it's more important to be responsible with your time and talent than it is to get 100 on a test. It means if you need to study to learn the material, you spend the time doing the work and don't cheat or cut corners. Be responsible with that smart mind of yours!

Finally, don't use all your mental energy worrying about your grades when you could use that energy to sit down and do the work instead. Study, read, listen, and learn. When you are responsible with your time and your mind, you can trust that God is never worried about the final grade.

You can trust God.

Answer

GOD'S MORE CONCERNED WITH YOUR CHARACTER AND HEART THAN A PERFECT REPORT CARD. BEING RESPONSIBLE WITH YOUR SCHOOLWORK MATTERS, BUT DON'T LET FEAR ABOUT GRADES TAKE OVER.

QUESTION 64

WHAT IF I WANT PEOPLE TO LIKE ME?

Welcome one another, just as Christ also welcomed you, to the glory of God.—Romans 15:7

You crack a joke in class and no one laughs. You invite friends over after school and no one shows. What do you do when you start to feel like no one likes you?

I hope none of these things happen to you, but I also know they easily can. What I want you to know, however, is silence after your joke or friends not showing up doesn't mean you're not liked or loved. I hope you feel confident in who God made you to be and that you don't spend too much time wondering if everyone wants to be your friend.

I totally understand why you want everyone to like you, but not even Jesus was liked by everybody! If you let your mind spin and spin about being liked all the time, you'll never truly relax into who God made you to be.

The truth is you can spend time thinking about how everyone feels about you, *or* you can turn your thoughts around and think more about how you interact with and treat other people.

Be respectful to everyone around you. Seek out those who seem lonely and left out. Forgive others quickly. Support your friends in good times and comfort them in hard times. This is how Jesus acted, and He can help us live this way too.

When you live the way Jesus did—with love, compassion, and concern for others—you will start to notice that people want to be around you. Do you know why? They see something different about you! And that difference is Jesus.

You can trust God.

ANSWER

FOCUS ON TREATING PEOPLE HOW JESUS WOULD TREAT THEM. THEY WILL NOTICE AND BE DRAWN TO YOU.

QUESTION 65

WHAT IF I HAVE A BAD DAY?

So we do not focus on what is seen, but on what is unseen.
For what is seen is temporary, but what is unseen is eternal.
—2 Corinthians 4:18

The Bible has a lot of stories about people having bad days, so when you have a day when nothing is going right, you're not alone. Have you heard of some of these?

- When Daniel was put in a lion's den (Daniel 6)

- When Shadrach, Meshach, and Abednego were thrown in a fire (Daniel 3)

- When David faced the giant Goliath (1 Samuel 17)

- When Jonah got swallowed by a big fish (Jonah 1)

- When Ruth's husband died and she was left poor (Ruth 1)

- When Joseph's brothers sold him into slavery (Genesis 37)

- When Esther learned Haman was planning to murder her people (Esther 3–4)

- When Paul was thrown into prison, again (Acts 23–24)

Each of these people in the Bible had a bad day. Can you imagine any of these things happening to you? How scary, right? But do you know who comes through in every single one of those stories? God!

On your bad days, you may not face a giant, a lion, or a murderer, but you'll still face hard things. So, when you fail a test, your parents don't understand you, or the girl you like keeps ignoring you, remember bad days don't stay bad forever. Take a look at today's verse to remember that what you see is just temporary.

The Bible is one big story of God showing up for His people. On the good days and the bad days, you have a God who is right there with you—for all of it.

You can trust God.

ANSWER

THE BIBLE SAYS GOD'S MERCIES ARE NEW EVERY MORNING, EVEN ON A BAD DAY! HE WILL ALWAYS SHOW UP AND CAN HELP YOU FIND THE GOOD.

QUESTION 66

WHAT IF EVERYTHING IS CHANGING?

Don't worry about anything, but in everything, through prayer and petition with thanksgiving, present your requests to God. And the peace of God, which surpasses all understanding, will guard your hearts and minds in Christ Jesus.—Philippians 4:6–7

When you see a pile of leaves gathered in a yard in the fall, does it make you want to just run and jump right in it? I love the beautiful leaves in the fall. I live in Tennessee, and we have an amazing display of colorful trees that time of year! But as fall turns to winter, those yellow, orange, and red leaves make their way to the ground, and we start a whole new season—a cold and often gray one.

Changing leaves may be pretty, but change in our lives can be hard to handle.

It might be a new school, new friends, new town—or maybe it's not even such big things! Maybe small changes are adding up: You started playing lacrosse on a new team or you joined a new class at church. Your sister is off to high school, so you won't see her in the hallway anymore. One of your parents takes a new job, so you have more chores to do around the house.

Whatever it may be, change can make you feel like everything around you is moving and you can't find your footing.

Did you know God cares about every part of that? When everything is changing, He's not upset to hear what you think about it. You can take every request, every prayer, and every worry to Him. He can be your steady ground. Ask Him to help you learn the names of the people in your new class. Ask Him to help you get through the school day without your sister. Tell Him when you're scared or excited or don't even know what to feel.

You can trust God.

ANSWER

IN THE MIDDLE OF A LOT OF CHANGE, GOD WILL BE YOUR STEADINESS AND YOUR CONSTANT. HE NEVER CHANGES!

QUESTION 67

WHAT IF SOMETHING HAPPENS TO MY FAMILY?

I call to God, and the LORD will save me.—Psalm 55:16

My favorite movie as a kid was *The Lion King* (and in my day we only had the cartoon version). I could barely watch the scene where Mufasa dies though! It broke my heart every single time (still does!).

Movies and TV shows are fun to watch, but sometimes they put scenarios in our heads that make us think the same thing might happen to us. When we see someone die during a movie, it not only makes us sad, but we start to wonder, *Is that going to happen to my family?*

Sometimes questions like this are just hypothetical, meaning an imaginary situation, but other times they are rooted in reality. Maybe one of your parents has a dangerous job or is battling an illness. Whatever the case, what-if scenarios can be overwhelming. But God can help you through every part of that.

A great first step is to think about what's real. If you're having a nightmare because of a scene in a movie (not real) or you've stressed yourself out over an idea (not real), ask God to help you stay present with what's going on here and now instead. Pray: *God, show me what is true and real today.*

Second, if a family member is in a situation that makes you nervous (real), take it to God. Ask Him to protect your mom, dad, brother, or sister. Pray: *God, will You protect my _____ and keep them safe? Will You also slow down my mind and give me peace?*

There is nothing you or your family will face that God has not seen before, and there's nothing you fear that He can't guide you through.

You can trust God.

ANSWER

GOD HEARS EVERY ONE OF YOUR PRAYERS. HE HEARS THE ONES YOU'RE PRAYING AS THE DAY BEGINS AND THE ONES YOU'RE WHISPERING INSIDE WHEN YOU'RE REALLY SCARED. HE'S A PROTECTOR. HE'S GOT YOU.

QUESTION 68

WHAT IF I'M NOT AS GOOD AT EVERYTHING?

Now as we have many parts in one body, and all the parts do not have the same function, in the same way we who are many are one body in Christ and individually members of one another.—Romans 12:4–5

I'm not fast enough. I'm not smart enough. He's more likable than me. My parents like her more.

When you start comparing yourself to others, you plant a lie in your head about who you are. You will start seeing yourself as less than others. It's like putting on glasses that give you blurry vision, and then you can no longer see yourself (or anything) clearly because you are too worried about not being good enough.

Starting now, I hope you will fight the urge to compare yourself to other guys. It will save you so much heartache in years to come. I want you to see yourself the way God sees you and live confidently in that—not bragging about yourself, but trusting in the reality that God made you unique, unlike anyone else.

If every single person looked the same, wore the same thing, and acted the same way, you would never get to see the creativity of God! You couldn't celebrate diversity. God painted a beautiful masterpiece when He made you, and your colors stand out on their own! Take off the comparison glasses so you can see your true colors clearly.

You can trust God.

ANSWER

WHO GETS TO DEFINE IF YOU'RE GOOD ENOUGH? ONLY GOD. WHAT HE MADE WAS GOOD, AND HE MADE YOU.

QUESTION 69

WHAT IF I'M SCARED TO TALK TO GOD?

May the Lord of peace himself give you peace always in every way.—2 Thessalonians 3:16

When you walk up to your friend and start a conversation, do you struggle to know what to say? I'm guessing you don't! You enjoy telling your friend about a video you watched or how you felt about that test yesterday, and your friend enjoys hearing about your life and all that's going on. If you're worried about how to pray to God, just think about it like you're talking to your friend!

Even though God is your Father and your King and deserves your worship, respect, and gratitude, you can tell Him anything and everything. You don't have to be scared about saying the right words or reciting anything specific. Just tell Him what's on your mind! And if you don't know what to say, you can turn to Matthew 6:9–13 where Jesus taught us how to pray.

Sometimes when I'm so overwhelmed that I don't know how to pray, I just say Jesus's name over and over again because His name is calming. When we call Jesus's name, He knows what we need and how to answer our prayers even when we don't know how to pray (Romans 8:26). You can even repeat verses from the Bible to help you get started with your prayer: "My help comes from the Lᴏʀᴅ" (Psalm 121:2).

The next time you're worried about praying the "right" way, remember that you know the God of the universe and He calls you friend. He's not a cartoon character or a made-up legend. He's Jesus—your God, your Creator, your Savior, your Friend.

You can trust God.

Answer

Just talk to God. Prayers don't have to be fancy or long. Say His name. Tell Him what's on your mind. Ask Him for what you need.

QUESTION 70

WHAT IF I'M TIRED OF BEING BRAVE?

"Be strong and courageous; don't be terrified or afraid of them. For the LORD your God is the one who will go with you; he will not leave you or abandon you."—Deuteronomy 31:6

Brave. It's a word I kind of like but kind of don't want to like. Here's why: I think brave people are cool! I admire them. When tough things come their way, they seem to take a deep breath and just go for it.

But here's the thing. Looking brave and being brave are not the same. You may appear to be brave when you make it through getting a shot without crying (and it's okay if you don't!), but the reality is you may be terrified on the inside.

Bravery comes from God, and He can make you brave. The truth is, you're going to face some days when you need strength and you need bravery. Maybe there's a new zip line at camp and you need a little courage to jump off the edge! Or maybe you need a lot of bravery during a hospital stay, a funeral, or a big move.

And there might be times when you're tired of trying to be brave. Let me remind of you this: In any moment, big or small, when everything's too overwhelming or painful, God is with you.

When a doctor's office feels like the place where everything hurts . . .

When the needle pricks and pokes won't stop . . .

When you need someone to hold your hand . . .

You can be brave because God makes you brave.

When the moving truck is on the way . . .

When you're headed to camp and you don't know anyone else who will be there . . .

When someone's explaining what will happen at the funeral . . .

You can be strong because God makes you strong.

He will give you what you need. He will carry you through. You can trust God.

ANSWER

YOUR BRAVERY COMES FROM GOD. ON THE DAYS WHEN YOU AREN'T SURE HOW TO FIND THE COURAGE, REMEMBER YOU DON'T HAVE TO FIND IT ON YOUR OWN. GOD WILL PROVIDE.

ACTIVITY DAY

Find a basketball and a hoop, and play a game of "Trust." Every time the ball goes in the hoop, shout out one thing that is true about God. For example:

God is good.

God is a protector.

God is always with me.

If you don't have a basketball or hoop anywhere near you, make one. Use any ball you can find (or crumple up some paper). For the hoop, you can use a laundry basket, trash can, or maybe even the bathtub!

If you can't think of things to say when you make a basket, start spelling out the word *trust* instead. T-R-U-S-T!

ANSWER RECAP

- Being different is not a bad thing. You are loved for who you are, and you belong to God.

- God always has a plan. Trust that He's going to take care of your parents and your family.

- God's more concerned with your character and heart than a perfect report card. Don't let fear about grades take over.

- Focus on treating people how Jesus would treat them. They will notice and be drawn to you.

- The Bible says God's mercies are new every morning, even on a bad day!

- In the middle of a lot of change, God will be your constant. He never changes!

- God hears every one of your prayers. He's a protector. He's got you.

- Only God gets to define you. What He made was good, and He made you.

- Prayers do not have to be fancy or long. Just talk to God. Say His name. Tell Him what's on your mind.

- Your bravery comes from God. Remember you don't have to find courage on your own. God will provide.

QUESTION 71

WHAT IF I'M DREADING SOMETHING?

When I am filled with cares, your comfort brings me joy.
—Psalm 94:19

I have a confession: I really don't like going to the dentist. Growing up, I never wanted to admit that because my aunt Helen was my dental hygienist and the dentist, Dr. Ted, was the friendliest man you'll ever meet. Still, I dreaded going every time. I didn't like having my teeth cleaned or getting a filling. The only good part about it was picking something fun from the treasure box at the end. I always went for the sugar-free gum . . . until I had braces!

Do you ever feel the dread of something creeping in the night before, the day before, even the week before the thing is scheduled to happen? I used to feel that way before going to the dentist. This feeling can turn your days upside down, and sometimes you don't even realize why. You carry the negative emotions around with you, often not realizing they don't have anything to do with what's happening today. Instead, they're connected to the things you're dreading in the future.

When you notice those negative feelings, ask God to replace them with joy.

The truth is, the anticipation of going to the dentist was often worse than actually being there! As soon as I walked into the office, I'd see all the familiar faces, catch up with my aunt, and (despite the uncomfortable cleaning in the middle) be well on my way to a new toothbrush and treat from the treasure box. The dentist's office held some smiles for me after all.

God can give you joy when you think it's not possible. He loves to do that! He's a God of comfort and light, and He can change your dread into delight.

You can trust God.

ANSWER

ASK GOD TO SHOW YOU AT LEAST ONE GOOD THING ABOUT WHATEVER IT IS YOU'RE DREADING. FINDING SOMETHING TO BE THANKFUL FOR CAN CHANGE YOUR ATTITUDE.

QUESTION 72
WHAT IF I'M ALONE?

Therefore, we may boldly say, The Lord is my helper; I will not be afraid. What can man do to me?—Hebrews 13:6

One of my favorite Christmas movies is *Home Alone*. Have you seen it? I won't spoil anything, but the adventure that Kevin McCallister experiences when his family accidentally leaves him at home during their Christmas vacation is a fun roller coaster of emotions.

But I can't imagine what it would be like to actually be left behind as a young kid, all alone. I don't think I would be as resourceful and skilled as Kevin was in the movie. I'm pretty sure I would panic. What about you?

I have spent a lot of time alone as an adult, and I can tell you, sometimes it's great, sometimes it's lonely, and sometimes it's scary. But here's what I've learned in those moments:

I'm not alone. And neither are you.

You have a God who is always with you, and that's a promise (Isaiah 41:10). Just like you feel the wind but don't see it, you can feel God's presence even when you don't see Him in the room with you. And His presence changes everything.

When you are alone or you feel alone, trust that God is right there. He will not leave you, and He will not fail you. He is Emmanuel, which means "God with us," and that means "alone" never has to be your reality.

You can trust God.

Answer

Even if you feel completely alone and unnoticed, you are never on your own. God is always by your side.

QUESTION 73

WHAT IF MY FEELINGS ARE HURT?

Whoever conceals an offense promotes love, but whoever gossips about it separates friends.—Proverbs 17:9

You're not invited."

It makes my stomach turn upside down just thinking about those words. But I've heard them before, and maybe you have too.

Navigating hurt feelings with your friends can be hard. Boys can easily overlook each other, and friends might not realize how you're actually feeling.

I can't step in and tell you why your friend said what he said, but I can tell you that you're loved no matter what.

Talk about it with your friends, though! Approach them with kindness and ask questions. Attempt to have a conversation about what's going on with your friendship, and let each other share and listen. Many times, it's just a disagreement that you need to talk through. Other times your friend has been really hurt by something you didn't even know you did, and you need to hear him out.

When this is the case, you can ask God to guide you through the hard conversation. If you're a Christian, He's given you the Holy Spirit to live within you as your Counselor. He can nudge you when it's time to speak and when it's time to listen. He can help you admit when you are wrong. He can help heal hurt feelings and friendships.

Ultimately, if a friendship ends, it will be sad for a while, and you will be okay. Friends will come and go, but God will remain by your side.

You can trust God.

ANSWER

HURT FEELINGS CAN STING, BUT THEY DON'T DEFINE YOUR VALUE. REMEMBER WHO MADE YOU (GOD!), AND LET HIM HELP YOU WORK ON FRIENDSHIPS.

Question 74

What If I Get Homesick?

"I will be the same until your old age, and I will bear you up when you turn gray. I have made you, and I will carry you; I will bear and rescue you."—Isaiah 46:4

Today's topic was supposed to be about when you get homesick and miss your friends and family. But you know what? As I'm writing this, I'm sitting in a cabin that some generous friends let me borrow for the weekend, and *I'm* the one who's homesick. Yep, me! I'm an adult who thought going away alone to write would be fun (and don't get me wrong, it is!), but I quickly realized it was lonely too.

It's okay to miss your people. It's nothing to be embarrassed about. And when I say, "your people," I mean your closest family and friends. You love them! They're important to you. For example, have you ever gone to a sleepover or an overnight camp and things felt unfamiliar and uncomfortable because your mom and dad weren't there to say good night, or your best friend wasn't right next to you? That feeling is normal.

When your heart is sad because you wish you were with your family or friends, try praying these three things. (And I'm going to do the same in my cabin!)

1. Thank God for your people. Mention them by name.

2. Ask God to give you peace right where you are while you're away from them.

3. Ask God to help you love those around you (and even make new friends).

Finally, trust in the fact that just as God can be with you at all times, He can be with your family and friends too. You're okay with Him, and so are they.

You can trust God.

ANSWER

IT'S OKAY TO BE HOMESICK AND MISS YOUR FAMILY AND FRIENDS. IT SHOWS HOW MUCH YOU LOVE THEM! ASK GOD TO HELP YOU BE PRESENT AND ENJOY WHERE YOU ARE UNTIL YOU SEE YOUR PEOPLE AGAIN.

QUESTION 75

WHAT IF I CAN'T FALL ASLEEP?

Those who trust in the LORD will renew their strength; they will soar on wings like eagles; they will run and not become weary, they will walk and not faint.—Isaiah 40:31

The other night I heard a weird noise in my house that I had never heard before. Of course, my thoughts started racing. *What was that? Did that come from downstairs or upstairs? Did I really hear it, or am I crazy?* I was trying to think through every scenario while also telling myself it was nothing. I still have no idea what I heard, but my mind was in full-on amusement park mode, swirling and twirling and keeping me from falling asleep.

It's frustrating when you can't fall asleep when you want to, isn't it? I know people say to count sheep in your head, but does that actually work? At first, I'm just frustrated I can't go to sleep. Then worry starts creeping in that if I never fall asleep, I won't be able to stay awake tomorrow. Have you been there? The thing is—the faster you can calm your mind, the better. When your worry starts running away with what-ifs, you end up sitting on that never-ending Ferris wheel instead of hopping off and finally falling asleep.

When I can't sleep, I talk to God. It calms me no matter what. I spent a lot of years feeling terrible if I accidently fell asleep while praying to Him, but one day I realized He considers it a joy for me to talk to Him and rest in Him.

You know the God who gives you strength. Talk to Him at night and trust Him to carry you through the day, no matter how much energy you have.

You can trust God.

Answer

Whether your mind is racing or you're just not tired, it's going to be okay. Sleep will come soon, and God can give you energy when you need it.

QUESTION 76

WHAT IF I'M DISAPPOINTED?

Humble yourselves, therefore, under the mighty hand of God, so that he may exalt you at the proper time, casting all your cares on him, because he cares about you.—1 Peter 5:6–7

Your parents said no to you going to a friend's birthday party this weekend.

You didn't get the part you wanted in the play.

Your cast isn't coming off in time to try out for the swim team.

None of your friends are in your new class.

Different things disappoint us all the time. We have an idea of how we want things to go—how we see our weekend going or what we want to do after school—and when reality doesn't live up to the expectation, we feel all kinds of emotions. We might be mad or annoyed or sad. And whether the disappointment is over a big thing or a small thing, it can really mess with our day and our mind.

God notices your disappointments. He cares when you're mad your friend went to another birthday party instead of yours. He cares when you're frustrated your dad couldn't be at your game. He cares when you're upset the movie you wanted to see is sold out. And He cares when you're disappointed about big things too.

Your feelings matter to God. They're not a burden on Him, and it's okay to admit what you feel. In the Bible, 1 Peter 5:7 reminds us, "[Cast] all your cares on him, because he cares about you." You don't have to keep all your disappointments to yourself. God is big enough and strong enough to hold them for you—and He wants to.

You can trust God.

ANSWER

IT'S OKAY TO BE DISAPPOINTED ABOUT THINGS, AND IT'S OKAY TO TELL GOD ABOUT IT. IN TIME, HE CAN TURN YOUR SADNESS INTO JOY AGAIN.

QUESTION 77

WHAT IF MY FEELINGS ARE OUT OF CONTROL?

God is not a God of disorder but of peace.—1 Corinthians 14:33

I know that sometimes when an adult asks you, "How are you?" it's hard to give an answer. The easy thing to do is say, "Fine." The hard thing to do is really think about how you're feeling on the inside.

Your emotions can often make you feel out of control, because they can come on quickly and you can feel more than one. You might not even realize what you're feeling or how you're acting. For example, let's say a friend who moved away last year has been planning to visit you this weekend, but he ended up getting sick and had to cancel at the last minute. Soon after you hear the news, your mom asks if you have any homework. You answer in a short way with some attitude, and when she questions you about the attitude and asks if you're okay, you yell back. Now she's mad, you're mad, and you're not even sure why.

Deep down, the sadness you were feeling about your friend came out as anger at your mom. It's crazy how our emotions can take over!

This craziness may make you feel out of control and make your mind spiral, but there are a few things you can ask God to do in those moments.

- Ask God to help stop your mind from running away with your worries, and ask Him to help you calm any anger or other strong feelings.

- Take a deep breath and think about what you're feeling deep inside. Maybe even consider going somewhere quiet for a minute to think or move your body (walk, run, shoot a basketball) to work out the emotions.

- If you can name what you're feeling, tell someone! Then ask God to help you through those feelings.

You have a Helper. God does not leave you alone to figure out hard moments and feelings all by yourself.

It's okay to feel sad or mad, but what you do with those feelings matters. Trust that God will bring steadiness to the out-of-control feeling.

You can trust God.

Answer

ASK GOD TO BRING ORDER AND CALM TO ANY EMOTION THAT FEELS OUT OF CONTROL. HE'S SPLIT SEAS IN HALF, WALKED ON WATER, CALMED STORMS, AND WALKED OUT OF A GRAVE. HE'S CAPABLE.

QUESTION 78
WHAT IF I'M NERVOUS?

Protect me, God, for I take refuge in you.—Psalm 16:1

Having to give a speech or presentation in front of your class.

Singing a solo.

Taking a standardized test.

Getting ready for your first game.

Going to the doctor.

So many things can make you nervous, and honestly, reading through that list makes my stomach jump! Do any of these events make you anxious? What's not on this list that makes your stomach turn?

Being in the spotlight, preparing to do something new, or putting all your preparation into one big day can make anybody—even the most daring among us—get a little sweaty and anxious, and that's okay! Being strong is a great thing, but it's also okay to admit when you're nervous.

What I love about God is that He can bring a steadiness to a shaky-feeling day. Often the biggest source of your nerves is that you feel alone. So when your voice is trembling as you start to give your speech or you're short of breath when you step onto the field, find your safe place in God.

A little bit of nervousness won't hurt you, but when it keeps you from sleeping at night, focusing during the day, or feeling well overall, talk to God about it. God is bigger than your nerves and fear; He can protect you. No matter how the test, game, or presentation turns out, He is more than capable of carrying you through.

You can trust God.

ANSWER

BEING NERVOUS ABOUT SOMETHING IS TOTALLY NORMAL, BUT YOU DON'T HAVE TO CARRY IT BY YOURSELF. GOD CAN CARRY IT FOR YOU AND HELP YOU CALM THE NERVES. HE WANTS TO DO THAT FOR YOU.

QUESTION 79

WHAT IF EVERYTHING IS TOO SERIOUS?

A joyful heart is good medicine.—Proverbs 17:22

Do you ever hear someone laughing and giggling for so long that you start laughing too? You don't even know how it starts, but suddenly you're full-on belly laughing, tears starting to form in your eyes. It's the best feeling, right? You laugh so hard your stomach hurts!

When things get too serious and you get all worked up and worried about something, you might just need to laugh a little to relieve the stress. In fact, the Bible tells us that a joyful heart is good medicine. That's a type of medicine I want! Don't you?

Think about this too: If someone else is having a really hard day, what could you do to help them smile or laugh? If your friend is nervous about a doctor's appointment or an upcoming performance, you can help bring a smile to their face with a joke or funny story. Your humor can help relieve the stress and worry.

Sometimes the fun comes by going outside to play. Go find a swing. Run through the sprinklers. Climb a tree. Let the fresh air blow away the seriousness.

Laughing can calm your mind and bring joy to your heart. It puts a smile on your face and other people's too. It may seem like the oddest thing to do when life is really serious, but a break from all the heavy things can remind you that joy exists and that life won't always be this tough. Such hope comes from God, and it's what you need.

You can trust God.

ANSWER

LOOK FOR THE FUN IN THE MIDDLE OF THE SERIOUS. FIND SOMETHING TO LAUGH ABOUT AND SOMEWHERE TO PLAY. THINGS WON'T BE SERIOUS FOREVER.

QUESTION 80

WHAT IF I DISAGREE WITH SOMEONE?

Remind them of these things, and charge them before God not to fight about words. This is useless and leads to the ruin of those who listen.—2 Timothy 2:14

When you disagree with someone, how does it make you feel? Angry? Nervous about what they think of you? Unsure how to handle it? A disagreement in the movies often leads to big fight scenes. The swords come out or the fists go up. The intensity goes from zero to a hundred quickly, and all of a sudden everything is chaotic.

When you see how disagreements blow up in the movies, you might think that's how they will go in real life too. Because of that, you could begin to worry about having a different opinion from someone else. Let's say you and a friend are watching a football game. You agree with the referee's call, but your friend thinks it's wrong. Can you kindly disagree? Disagreements don't have to end in fights, and they don't have to end friendships.

When you think about it, lots of people disagreed with Jesus. As He traveled and taught, many people believed His teachings were wrong. Many questioned Him. It was Jesus's actions and response that mattered, however. He always responded with kindness and humility. He spoke the truth, but He did it in a loving way. You can do that too!

Whether you're disagreeing over something really big or really small, do so in a way that still respects the other person. If you're a Christian, you don't have to be afraid of conflict because you have the Holy Spirit living in you. He provides you with self-control, patience, and kindness. If you feel anger stirring within you, ask for help from your Helper! Jesus was our example, and you can live like He did, because He lives in you.

You can trust God.

ANSWER

IT'S OKAY TO DISAGREE, BUT CAN YOU DO IT WHILE STILL LOVING AND CARING FOR THE OTHER PERSON? IT'S POSSIBLE! STUDY HOW JESUS DID IT. PEOPLE DISAGREED WITH HIM ALL THE TIME.

ACTIVITY DAY

Let's build a fort.

You can make it as big or as small as you would like (or as your parents would like). Use Lego's or use pillows and boxes. Build yourself a fort for protection, and make a flag to add to the top. Write Psalm 16:1 on the flag. Look it up in your Bible or go look back at Question 78 to see what it says!

ANSWER RECAP

- Ask God to show you at least one good thing about whatever it is you're dreading.

- Even if you feel completely alone and unnoticed, God is always by your side.

- Remember who made you (God!), and let Him help you work on friendships.

- When you're homesick, ask God to help you enjoy where you are until you see your people again.

- If you can't fall asleep, it's going to be okay. Sleep will come soon, and God can give you energy when you need it.

- It's okay to be disappointed about things, and it's okay to tell God about it.

- Ask God to bring order and calm to any emotion that feels out of control.

- Being nervous about something is totally normal. God can help you calm the nerves.

- Look for the fun in the middle of the serious.

- It's possible to disagree while still loving and caring for the other person.

QUESTION 81

WHAT IF I'M SCARED OF STORMS?

He got up, rebuked the wind, and said to the sea, "Silence! Be still!"
The wind ceased, and there was a great calm. Then he said to them,
"Why are you afraid? Do you still have no faith?" And they were
terrified and asked one another, "Who then is this? Even the wind
and the sea obey him!"—Mark 4:39–41

Do you ever think a thunderstorm sounds like someone bowling in the sky? To me, the slow rumbling sounds like an eight-pound bowling ball making its way down the lane and crashing into the pins with a loud, crackling BOOM.

Watching a bowling ball knock over pins is fun and exciting, even with the final boom, but hearing a shocking clap of thunder can definitely be startling. One noise I expect. The other? Surprises me every time.

Storms can be loud and scary, and it's okay if they make you nervous! It's totally normal to be scared of something you can't control (like the weather).

Have you ever wondered how Jesus felt about storms? Mark 4 tells us. Jesus was in a boat with the disciples, who were acting like we'd expect people caught in a storm to act: they were freaking out! Jesus, on the other hand, was fast asleep.

The disciples woke up Jesus, asking, "Don't you care that we're going to die?" (Mark 4:38). Jesus then commanded the sea and storm to be still. Both came to a stop.

How was Jesus able to sleep during a storm that was crazy enough to make the disciples think they would die? He had such peace because He is the Son of God. This Jesus, the One who sleeps through and controls storms, is with us when the storms of life are happening around us.

Sometimes these storms are the weather-in-the-sky kind. But your storms might also be failing at the sport you want to be good at, constantly fighting with your brother, or struggling with a learning disability.

I won't tell you that Jesus will calm every storm you are in. But I do know He will sit with you in it. Comfort is found not just when the storm goes away. You can find comfort in the middle of a storm by being with Jesus. He is capable of calming the storm, but He's also capable of calming you. He will not leave you. He will not let you go. His peaceful presence changes everything.

You can trust God.

ANSWER

DURING A STORM, TRY TO THINK PAST THE NOISE AND TALK TO GOD ABOUT IT. ASK HIM TO KEEP YOU SAFE AND MAKE THE STORM GO AWAY. HE HEARS YOU. HE'S LISTENING.

Question 82

What If I Don't Want to Grow Up?

In him we have boldness and confident access through faith in him.—Ephesians 3:12

Have you seen the movies *Peter Pan* or *Hook*? Peter and the Lost Boys are stuck in their childhood years, which looks like a ton of fun when they're having food fights and playing in the forest all the time. But you find out later that it's not always all fun and games for them.

What do you think about growing up? Maybe there's something you really want to do, like try out for a middle school team, that you can't wait to get to. Or maybe there's something you're really nervous about, like getting a driver's permit, that you'd like to hold off on.

New responsibilities can be both exciting and intimidating. It's all new, and sometimes there's a lot of pressure to live up to the expectations you think everyone is putting on you. Does it ever make you want to stay a kid and not grow up?

It's totally normal. Even as an adult, I sometimes wish I didn't carry all the responsibilities that I do, but growing up also comes with learning and experiencing so many things! The best part is that God leads you through every step of the way. You won't be left on your own to figure everything out. You have a Good Father to follow, and He walks with you through every new milestone, permit test, and job application. You are not alone.

You can trust God.

ANSWER

AS YOU GROW UP, YOU WON'T BE ALONE. GOD HAS A PLAN FOR YOU, AND HE IS ALWAYS WITH YOU, YOUNG OR OLD.

QUESTION 83

WHAT IF THE NEXT STEP IS HARD?

The Lord my Lord is my strength; he makes my feet like those of a deer and enables me to walk on mountain heights!—Habakkuk 3:19

Have you ever seen a deer? I often see them at one of my favorite places to walk in Nashville—Radnor Lake. When I head into the wooded hills surrounding the lake, I typically spot them hanging out a little way off the trail, keeping watch on who's walking by while they enjoy a forest snack.

The hills around Radnor Lake aren't too high, but it wouldn't matter to the deer. On hills or mountains, those guys can stand up without stumbling. They're sure-footed. Isn't that cool? If you or I were standing on the side of tall mountain, we'd have to hold on to something or hunch over to make sure we wouldn't fall. But not deer. They can stand up easily, and they can stay steady.

I know there are days when you feel like you're struggling to stand up because you're not sure what to do next. Maybe you're torn over a big decision. Maybe you know you need to speak up about something but lack the courage. Maybe you need to end a friendship that isn't good for you. Whatever is bothering you, remember today's verse.

God makes you strong. He can give you steady feet like a deer and help you easily walk up whatever mountain you're trying to climb.

When you don't know what to do, turn to God. Nothing is too big or too scary for Him. He can give you the strength, wisdom, and sure-footedness you need to take a tough step forward.

He's just that good.

You can trust God.

ANSWER

THE COURAGE, BRAVERY, OR WISDOM YOU NEED CAN ALL BE FOUND IN GOD. HE CAN HELP YOU MAKE A DECISION AND TAKE THE NEXT STEP WHEN IT FEELS HARD.

QUESTION 84

WHAT IF I'M SCARED TO ASK GOD?

If any of you lacks wisdom, he should ask God—who gives to all generously and ungrudgingly—and it will be given to him. But let him ask in faith without doubting. For the doubter is like the surging sea, driven and tossed by the wind.—James 1:5–6

When my friend was a kid, she used to have a "question quota" from her parents. This meant she was allowed to ask a certain number of questions a day. She loved to talk (still does!) and has always been curious, but she had so many questions that her parents gave her a limit!

We often approach God with this same mindset—that our what-ifs or doubts or opinions might be too much for Him and there is a limit to what we can ask. However, when we stop ourselves from going to God, that increases our anxiety and ability to trust Him all the more!

In the Bible, we can read about person after person asking God questions or asking Jesus questions while He was on earth. They wanted to know how to live. They wanted to know when they would receive what they were promised. They wanted to know if Jesus could heal them. Plenty of the questions people asked in the Bible are the same ones we still ask today.

And you know what? God never turned His back on His people or cut off their questions.

You can ask God anything. He's not afraid of your questions or your feelings. He doesn't have a question quota.

Waiting for answers requires patience, though. God may not answer the way you want Him to, or He may take a long time to answer. Be listening! As you pray, give Him a chance to respond. Open your Bible. God can speak to you through the words He's already given you in His Word. He welcomes your curiosity with open arms.

You can trust God.

ANSWER

GOD WILL NEVER GET TIRED OF HEARING FROM YOU. ASK HIM ANYTHING. OPEN YOUR BIBLE AND LOOK FOR ANSWERS. HE WANTS YOUR TIME, QUESTIONS, AND HEART.

QUESTION 85

WHAT IF I MADE A BIG MISTAKE?

All have sinned and fall short of the glory of God; they are justified freely by his grace through the redemption that is in Christ Jesus.
—Romans 3:23–24

Have you ever watched a video of a giant set of dominoes set up across a floor? One tap of the first domino triggers the whole line to fall, sending them all crashing into each other. Or maybe you've built your own line of dominoes or toys and sent them crashing all the way down the line.

Have you ever felt like making a big mistake is similar to dominoes falling one after the other? One thing leads to another, and suddenly you realize the mistake has a bigger impact than you thought.

You missed a goal during your soccer game from a spot on the field you'd practiced over and over, or you forgot to do those chores for your mom even after you put a sticky-note reminder on your door.

Listen: Mistakes happen. Bad grades happen. Losing a game happens.

It's okay to be sad or frustrated for a little bit, but don't stay that way too long. Don't let those emotions start turning into roadblocks where you start believing you can never score a goal, ace a test, or remember the words to a song.

God understands mistakes. He understands that the world is broken and no one is perfect. If we were perfect, we would have never needed a Savior to come save us. But we're people who make a lot of mistakes, and we still need Jesus every day. So, the next time you make a mistake, remember that this is what it means to be human, and thank God that you don't have to be perfect because Jesus already is.

You can trust God.

ANSWER

IT MIGHT FEEL LIKE ONE BIG MISTAKE IS GOING TO RUIN EVERYTHING, BUT GOD IS BIGGER THAN THAT. HE'S HOLDING THE WORLD, WHICH MEANS YOU CAN'T RUIN IT.

Question 86

What If I Hate That My Body Is Changing?

Don't you know that your body is a temple of the Holy Spirit who is in you, whom you have from God? You are not your own, for you were bought at a price. So glorify God with your body.
—1 Corinthians 6:19–20

Did your parents ever buy you a new pair of pants, and then a few weeks later, they were already too short? Or maybe one day you noticed that your voice started cracking? Your body changes all the time, and sometimes that can be both cool and frustrating. Getting taller, bigger, and stronger may feel like an accomplishment, but learning about shaving, needing a bigger shoe size all the time, and keeping up with when to put on deodorant can be annoying.

If you're worried about anything happening to your body as you grow and get older, know that God created your body to do this. It's not a mystery to Him, and it's not a mystery to your dad or brothers or other men around you who can help you through all the changes.

The Bible also says your body is a temple—meaning it's a holy place where God lives. Because of this, you should care about how you treat your body.

Your body's ever-changing size and shape doesn't have to be a scary discovery. You can trust that God designed your body to do exactly what it should, and He has given you the resources to take care of it.

The God who made seasons to change, seeds to become trees, and caterpillars to transform into butterflies made your body to change too.

You can trust God.

ANSWER

YOUR BODY WILL GROW AND CHANGE A TON. IT'S NORMAL, AND GOD MADE YOUR BODY TO DO THAT! IF IT MAKES YOU REALLY NERVOUS, ASK AN ADULT YOU TRUST FOR SOME ADVICE.

QUESTION 87

WHAT IF I CAN'T CALM DOWN BEFORE BED?

Finally brothers and sisters, whatever is true, whatever is honorable, whatever is just, whatever is pure, whatever is lovely, whatever is commendable—if there is any moral excellence and if there is anything praiseworthy—dwell on these things.—Philippians 4:8

Recently I watched my beloved Georgia Bulldogs win another National Championship title, making them back-to-back champions! I watched the game with my brother, sister-in-law, niece, and nephew, and it ended pretty late for a school night. We were all so excited and wired from the game that we had trouble falling asleep.

Do you ever have those kinds of nights? It might not be from an exciting game, but maybe you had friends over and you're still in such a great mood about it that you can't seem to get your mind to shut off. It can be so frustrating when you start to think about the hours of sleep you are starting to miss.

In the book of Philippians, Paul reminded the people of Philippi to dwell on things that were true, honorable, lovely, and commendable. Paul knew all too well that the things we set our minds on are what our hearts will beat to. He understood that this world is a rough place, but there is *always* something good to focus our attention on.

Whenever you can't calm down enough to sleep, what if you think through some of those true, honorable, lovely, and commendable things to help settle your mind a bit? Whether it's been a bad day or a great one, spending a few minutes answering these three questions may be the thing you need to help you slow down. *(Answer these questions out loud or write your answers down.)*

1. What is one thing you are grateful for today?

2. What's one thing you are proud of lately?

3. What is one true thing about God that you need to focus on?

Use these answers to help you calm down as you close out your day.

You can trust God.

ANSWER

USE THE QUIET BEFORE BED TO BE STILL AND SLOW YOUR MIND DOWN. USE IT AS A CHANCE TO THINK ABOUT WHAT YOU'RE GRATEFUL FOR RIGHT NOW.

QUESTION 88

WHAT IF GOD CHANGES HIS MIND ABOUT ME?

Today the Lord has affirmed that you are his own possession as he promised you, that you are to keep all his commands, that he will elevate you to praise, fame, and glory above all the nations he has made, and that you will be a holy people to the Lord your God as he promised.—Deuteronomy 26:18–19

When you're at a restaurant, staring at a menu, is it easy for you to decide what to order? Growing up, I had one thing I'd almost always choose off the menu: chicken fingers. Choosing wasn't hard for me then, but now that I'm older and have widened my food horizon, making a decision can be a challenge. I place my order with the waiter, but then I hear what my friend orders and want to change my mind. Does that ever happen to you?

We humans are fickle, which means we go back and forth all the time—on little things and big things. For example, even Jesus's closest friends couldn't fully decide about following Him. Three different times, Jesus's disciple Peter denied knowing Him to protect himself. Three times! Jesus even predicted this would happen, and it sounded like a crazy idea, but it turned out to be true.

But guess what? Jesus never changed His mind about Peter. Jesus continued to love him and serve him, so much so that He died on the cross for Peter's (and our) sins.

Do you ever wonder if God will change His mind about you? As a fickle human being, you will mess up. You might doubt God or deny Him. You might get mad at Him or ignore Him, but He won't ever turn His back on you. So don't let your sins or frustrations pull you away from God. He wants you to bring all that to Him. He wants it so badly that He sent Jesus to live on earth and die in your place so that you could have eternal life with Him.

You can stop worrying that God will walk away from you, because He is not capable of it.

You can trust God.

ANSWER

GOD WOULD NEVER CHANGE HIS MIND ABOUT YOU. HE MADE YOU AND LOVES YOU DEEPLY.

QUESTION 89

WHAT IF PEOPLE DON'T LIKE ME?

L<small>ORD</small>, you have searched me and known me.—Psalm 139:1

Have you ever walked outside to see a group of kids playing a game of street hockey, but no one invited you to join? You might be able to brush it off, but oftentimes that small thought of, *Do they like me?* creeps in. And sometimes that one small thought leads to bigger ones:

> *If those guys don't like me, no one will like me.*

> *Because a few people don't understand me, no one understands me.*

> *There must not be anything cool or likable about me.*

None of this is true!

The Bible says what's true about you even when you're not sure. Open your Bible. Ask for help finding verses that talk about what God thinks about you, like today's verse in Psalm 139:1.

Then take what you think about yourself and see if it matches what the Bible says. If it matches, it's true! If it doesn't match, it's a lie. Let's try a few:

I think: *No one cares what I think.*

The Bible says: "I have called you friends, because I have made known to you everything I have heard from my Father" (John 15:15).

I think: *No one is ever going to like me.*

The Bible says: "Am I now trying to persuade people, or God? Or am I striving to please people? If I were still trying to please people, I would not be a servant of Christ" (Galatians 1:10).

When you question who you are or what matters, go to the Bible. There you'll find what's true.

You can trust God.

ANSWER

SOMETIMES PEOPLE ARE MEAN OR LEAVE YOU OUT, BUT IT ISN'T A REFLECTION ON WHO YOU ARE. GOD DEFINES WHO YOU ARE.

QUESTION 90

WHAT IF I HAVE TO STAND UP FOR WHAT I BELIEVE IN?

"Love the Lord your God with all your heart, with all your soul, with all your mind, and with all your strength. The second is, Love your neighbor as yourself. There is no other command greater than these."—Mark 12:30–31

Have you ever been picked on for standing up for something you believed in? It doesn't feel very good, does it? It makes you feel all alone and might even make you question the thing you're standing up for.

Let's talk about Noah and the ark for a minute. Remember that story from Genesis 6 and 7? God gave Noah specific instructions on how to build a giant boat to hold his family and pairs of each animal on the earth. Because Noah did everything God said, they were all safe and sound on board the ark when the whole world flooded. Everything and everyone left behind was swept away by the water.

But think about all the days leading up to the flood. Noah must've spent years sawing and hammering. Although we don't know what the other people were thinking at the time, we can imagine they were curious why this six-hundred-year-old man was building a giant boat. They must have thought he was crazy!

God has asked us to do unpopular things. No, He hasn't commanded you to build a gigantic boat, but He has asked you to love Him with all your heart, soul, mind, and strength, and to love your neighbors as yourself. These are the main instructions for your life. Will you obey them without caring what other people think? Noah's obedience played a part in saving humanity. Who in your life might get to meet God because of your obedience to Him?

You can stand up for what you believe in and not worry about what others think because you are part of a bigger story: God's story.

You can trust God.

ANSWER

DOING WHAT GOD ASKS MAY NOT ALWAYS BE A POPULAR CHOICE. BUT FOLLOWING GOD AND BEING OBEDIENT TO HIM WILL ALWAYS BE REWARDED.

ACTIVITY DAY

Do some detective work.

What does the Bible say about being scared? We've talked about it off and on throughout this book, but I want to see what you can find.

Try starting with Psalm 23. Open your Bible, or ask an adult to help you pull up the Bible on a phone or tablet. Turn to Psalm 23 and read the whole thing. What do you learn about God from this chapter? How do the words help calm your fear and worry?

ANSWER RECAP

- During a storm, try to think past the noise and talk to God about it.

- As you grow up, you won't be alone. God has a plan for you, and He is always with you, young or old.

- The courage, bravery, or wisdom you need can all be found in God. He can help you take the next step when it feels hard.

- God will never get tired of hearing from you. Ask Him anything.

- It might feel like one big mistake is going to ruin everything, but God is bigger than that. He's holding the world.

- Your body will grow and change a ton. It's normal, and God made your body to do that!

- Use the quiet before bed as a chance to think about what you're grateful for right now.

- God will never change His mind about you. He made you and loves you deeply.

- Sometimes people are mean or leave you out, but it isn't a reflection on who you are. God defines who you are.

- Following God and being obedient to Him will always be rewarded.

QUESTION 91
WHAT IF HEAVEN IS NOT REAL?

As it is written, What no eye has seen, no ear has heard, and no human heart has conceived—God has prepared these things for those who love him.—1 Corinthians 2:9

Do you ever think about heaven? You probably haven't had to think about it unless someone you know has passed away. Those moments are so sad because you miss the person, but if they're in heaven, it's comforting to remember they are with God!

I think about heaven sometimes. I think about the people I'll see, what it will be like to worship God, and what everything will look like. Because I've never seen heaven, though, it can leave me with more and more questions. Do you feel that way? Maybe the idea of heaven makes you a little nervous because it seems like a big mystery. Maybe you even wonder if heaven is real (it is!).

The Bible gives us a sneak peek of what's to come. It says:

- God will make all things new—there will be a new heaven and a new earth (Revelation 21:1).

- We will have new bodies (Philippians 3:21).

- There will be no death, no sadness, and no pain (Revelation 21:4).

Can you imagine how incredible heaven will be? Your brothers and sisters in Christ will be there, all that is hard and broken will be restored, and we will get to worship God forever. We will never get bored, because we will be with our limitless God, who will make everything perfect again. Forever.

Think on these things the next time the thought of heaven makes you doubtful or anxious. God has given you the Bible to help you understand what eternity with Him will be like. And when I read all these reminders of what's to come, I can't wait!

God has prepared an amazing, better-than-you-can-imagine place for you.

You can trust God.

ANSWER

SOME THINGS MENTIONED IN THE BIBLE, LIKE HEAVEN, ARE SO BIG THAT OUR HUMAN BRAINS HAVE A HARD TIME UNDERSTANDING THEM. WE KNOW THE BIBLE IS TRUE, THOUGH, WHICH MEANS HEAVEN IS TOO, AND THAT IS EXTREMELY EXCITING NEWS.

QUESTION 92

WHAT IF I DON'T MATTER?

It was you who created my inward parts; you knit me together in my mother's womb. I will praise you because I have been remarkably and wondrously made. Your works are wondrous, and I know this very well.—Psalm 139:13–14

Someone asked me recently if I like celebrating my birthday. I do! It's not because I care about a huge party or lots of presents though. It's because it's the one day a year when people intentionally remind me that I matter to them. The cards, texts, phone calls, and kind words all help me remember I am loved, and it makes me really grateful for the people in my life.

Has anyone ever made you feel the opposite—like you didn't matter? People's words can cut deep, but we often spend too much time worrying about something mean someone has said to us or about us. We use those words to be harsh on ourselves, but that's the opposite of what God wants for us.

Your feelings are valid! Mean words are hard to forget, but they don't have the final say regarding who you are. God didn't forget anything when He made you. He didn't skip a step when creating your personality or forget to count the number of hairs on your head when designing your skin tone and hair texture (Luke 12:7). You might not understand (or even like) why

God made you how He did, but it's important to remember God made you on purpose and with a purpose.

The next time other people's mean words are ringing in your ears, open your Bible to Psalm 139. Read the whole thing, and ask God to show you why He made you. Remember that what God makes is special—every single time. Choose to think about the kind words people say about you on your birthday instead of other people's mean words.

You matter, and you can trust God.

ANSWER

IF ANYONE MAKES YOU FEEL LIKE YOU DON'T MATTER, REMEMBER THAT YOU MATTER TO GOD. YOU ARE UNIQUE AND CREATED FOR A PURPOSE.

QUESTION 93

WHAT IF I CAN'T STOP THINKING ABOUT IT?

Let your eyes look forward; fix your gaze straight ahead.
—*Proverbs 4:25*

When my nephew was younger and got his first watch, he was obsessed with telling us all what time it was, especially when the clock hit the top of the hour. Whenever we drove six hours to visit my parents (his grandparents), he would be sure to let us know each time his watch hit a new hour. "It's 10:00! It's 11:00! It's 12:00!"

The anticipation of something fun on the horizon will always make us check the date or the time. It's exciting, but it can be a little distracting at the same time. There is absolutely nothing wrong with being excited, but if dreaming and planning is getting in the way of focusing on what's going on right now, that's a problem.

When this happens to you, I suggest pulling out a journal to help. Give yourself a few minutes a day to write down what you're excited about and what you're thinking about. It's like your little window in the day to celebrate! Then, when you're done, close the journal and put it away. Use that as a visual reminder to focus on what's in front of you right now.

Sometimes you might be so excited about what's to come that you're restless and miss what God is doing in the present. As you journal, ask Him to take that hopeful joy you have about an upcoming event and help you feel it on your normal, everyday, run-of-the-mill days too. Your excited heart brings God joy, and He can give you that delight in life every single day.

You can trust God.

Answer

THANK GOD THAT YOU HAVE SOMETHING TO BE EXCITED ABOUT! THEN ASK HIM TO KEEP YOU FOCUSED ON THE DAY AHEAD. IT MAY SEEM LIKE A SMALL THING, BUT HE CARES ABOUT IT.

QUESTION 94

WHAT IF IT'S NOT WHAT I PLANNED?

We know that all things work together for the good of those who love God, who are called according to his purpose.—Romans 8:28

When COVID-19 hit in 2020 and schools started closing (then eventually went to virtual learning), I felt so bad for all of you. I knew none of you imagined your school year going that way. You expected to see your friends every day, talk to your teacher in person, and still have normal class parties and plays and sports. You had to get creative in staying connected to classmates, and you had to adjust your schedule and routine to fit the new plan you didn't ask for. How was that experience for you?

There will always be things that don't go according to your plans. The impact might not be as big as that of a global pandemic, but you will still have days you don't expect.

For example, when you think back on 2020, I bet you can remember some things you were grateful for, right? Maybe it was going on lots of family walks or being able to wear pajamas while you did your schoolwork. Maybe it was having more time to learn a new skill or video chat more with relatives who live far away.

When life doesn't go the way you planned, pointing out the good things can help shift your heart and mind. It can help you fight the fears of what's coming next and focus on what you know to be true.

God has a plan. Always. And when things aren't the way you imagined, you can start to worry that nothing will ever go right again. Fight against that lie. Look for the good things right in front of you. Thank God for them, and trust that yesterday, today, and tomorrow, He's working everything together for good.

You can trust God.

ANSWER

WHEN THINGS DON'T GO AS PLANNED, LOOK FOR THE GOOD. REMEMBER THAT GOD ALWAYS HAS A PLAN, AND HIS PLAN IS BETTER THAN OUR OWN.

QUESTION 95

WHAT IF I REGRET SOMETHING?

Forgetting what is behind and reaching forward to what is ahead, I pursue as my goal the prize promised by God's heavenly call in Christ Jesus.—Philippians 3:13–14

Have you ever struggled to get up in the morning because you regretted something you did the day before?

Many times I've lain in bed replaying conversations in my head, trying to figure out why I said or did something I shouldn't have. But it may not be something like that for you! Maybe you didn't invite an old friend to your laser-tag party, but his feelings are hurt, and now you regret it. Or perhaps you had to decide between playing golf and doing the robotics club, and you wish you could change your decision.

How do you handle regret?

It can be easy to let your mind go back over the thing you're missing out on or the thing you wish you hadn't done. This pattern might lead you to feel guilty or to feel bad about yourself. When you begin to replay those moments that fill you with regret, ask God to help you move forward and move past it.

Letting our minds run away with the things we wish we had done differently will only leave us thinking about the past all the time. As today's verse reminds us, we can forget what is behind and reach forward to what is ahead. Why? Because God makes everything new every single day (Lamentations 3:22–23).

God will help you overcome the regret.

You can trust God.

Answer

Thankfully you have a God who specializes in taking your regret and giving you hope instead.

QUESTION 96

WHAT IF I DON'T WANT TO BE HONEST?

Do not lie to one another, since you have put off the old self
with its practices and have put on the new self. You are being
renewed in knowledge according to the image of your Creator.
—Colossians 3:9–10

I can remember walking into my mom's room when I was about five years old, and she looked at me with a funny look, and said, "Did you cut your hair?" My eyes shifted because I couldn't look her in the eye, and I said, "No." But it was an obvious lie. A small section of my hair was clearly shorter than the rest, and I had been caught. Why did I cut my hair? I have no idea. But why did I lie about it? Well, I clearly wanted to avoid the consequences. What you probably already know, though, is that the consequences of lying are often harsher than just choosing to tell the truth from the start.

Why are you sometimes tempted to avoid telling the truth? Well, if your situation is similar to the one I was in, you don't want to get in trouble, so you try to hide the mistake. Other times, you don't want to be honest because you don't want the attention. If you're honest that you're truly struggling with reading, it means asking for help, and you don't want that.

All of it may be rooted in not wanting people to really see the true things going on in you. You don't want to be too much or do too much or give people a reason to give you extra attention. God knows and sees the true you at all times, and although that may feel intimidating, I hope it also feels like a relief! He loves and cares for you so much, despite your desire to hide. So be brave enough to be honest. Nothing you do is going to shock God or surprise Him, so you can run to Him for forgiveness and a safe place to land.

You can trust God.

ANSWER

GOD IS NOT SCARED OF THE TRUTH. HE ALREADY KNOWS WHAT'S GOING ON, AND HE LOVES YOU NO MATTER WHAT.

QUESTION 97

WHAT IF GOD ISN'T WHO HE SAYS HE IS?

Jesus said to them, "Truly I tell you, before Abraham was, I am."
—John 8:58

Have you ever felt like someone fooled you or betrayed you? If you've seen the movie *Thor*, think about Loki for a second. He's one of those people you think you can trust, but you quickly learn you can't. He's not the kind of guy everyone thinks he is.

When we feel like we've been fooled, lied to, or betrayed, we start to question other people around us, and we can easily wonder about God too. It's one thing to say we should trust Him, but how do we know we can?

When you're trying to figure out if you can trust someone, what do you do? You see if they keep their promises to you. You see if they follow through on what they say they will do. You ask other people if they trust this person. You look for the proof and consistency.

It's the same with God! The Bible is our source of proof about who God is, and we have full access to it! We don't have to wonder or guess; we have story after story of God keeping His promises and showing up for His people. We have eyewitnesses who saw Jesus, talked to Him, watched Him die on a cross, and saw Him alive again three days later. We have stories of miracles and changed lives, all written down in Scripture.

Those stories are your proof! That's how you know you won't be fooled, and this isn't a game. God—your Father, Creator, Protector, and Savior—is who He says He is. He will not fail you, and He will not leave you.

You can trust God.

Answer

The Bible is our greatest resource to show us the proof that God is real.

QUESTION 98

WHAT IF I'M TOO EXCITED TO SLEEP?

This is the day the LORD has made; let's rejoice and be glad in it.
—*Psalm 118:24*

Why does anyone expect us to sleep on Christmas Eve?

I don't know about your family traditions, but when I was growing up, we opened gifts and had a big family breakfast right away on Christmas morning. My brothers are a good bit older than I am, so they typically were hard to get out of bed. But I was up and ready to find my presents and see the look on my family's faces when they opened theirs too. I never slept well on Christmas Eve as a kid. The excitement was my late-night buddy.

Whether it's the night before your birthday, the big swim meet, or the first day of school, excitement and expectation can take control of your mind . . . so much so that you can't sleep a wink!

When this happens, try to remind yourself to *be present*. That means to focus on what's going on in each moment. And here's a tip: if it's *presents* you're excited to see the next day, think about what *being present* means right now. What are the gifts you can be grateful for in this moment?

If you're lying in bed, focus on the softness of your blankets and pillow. Take deep breaths. Listen to the quiet. Bring your mind back to falling asleep instead of letting it run away with future plans. When you get so excited about what's coming that you don't sleep at all, you find yourself exhausted on the day you've been waiting on for so long! Instead, here's what I suggest.

Focus on giving thanks: What can you thank God for now? What can you celebrate about today as you go to sleep?

Ask God to calm your mind and protect your joy. Remember, He can help you relax in the middle of your excitement.

You can trust God.

ANSWER

PRAY AS YOU GO TO BED. TALKING TO GOD WILL LIKELY CALM YOU DOWN AND HELP YOU FALL ASLEEP. PLUS, HE WANTS TO HEAR WHAT YOU'RE EXCITED ABOUT!

QUESTION 99

WHAT IF THE WORRY LASTS FOREVER?

You will keep the mind that is dependent on you in perfect peace, for it is trusting in you. Trust in the LORD forever, because in the LORD, the LORD himself, is an everlasting rock!—Isaiah 26:3–4

We've talked so much about all the what-if questions you have, and I wanted to tell you why it matters to me that you know you can trust God. I love the way your mind works, trying to figure out all the ins and outs of life, but when the questions turn into worry and fear, I want you to know who your steady Rock is.

Learning who God is—truly understanding His character, His goodness, His protection—can change the way you live. It can change the way you think. It can change what you do with your worry.

The things that make you scared and make you worry *will not last*.

God sent Jesus to save us because we couldn't save ourselves. Then He gave us the Holy Spirit, our Helper, to live in us! Jesus will return to earth one day and hit reset on it all, restoring it to the good, perfect way He intended it to be. The broken parts won't last.

But God does. He lives on forever, and you get to live with Him. As soon as you began a relationship with God, your forever life with Him began. He is with you now, which means you're protected. You have a Shepherd. You're not alone. You have a Rock. God is going behind you, in front of you, and beside you—now and always.

You can trust God.

ANSWER

THE WORRY WON'T LAST FOREVER BECAUSE GOD HAS ALREADY TAKEN CARE OF IT. HE WINS, WHICH MEANS YOU DO TOO.

Question 100

Can I Trust?

When I am afraid, I will trust in you. In God, whose word I praise, in God I trust; I will not be afraid. What can mere mortals do to me?—Psalm 56:3–4

Am I going to be okay? Am I good enough? Am I strong enough?

We worry about so many questions, and we've talked about a lot of them throughout this book. But I want to make sure you know one thing before you put this book away. It's the most important thing.

Jesus died for you, and you can trust Him.

I know we live in a world where we're constantly trying to figure out who can be trusted and what's real. In this book, I hope you discovered a God who had a plan for you before you were even born. He's a God who wins every battle. He's a God who has your back.

We are all born broken people—that includes you, me, your parents, and your friends. So if you're worried that you've messed up too much or you don't feel like you're enough, the truth is—none of us is enough without God.

God created people to be with Him, but because of our sinful and broken nature, we are all separated from God. On our own, we can do nothing to fix that. Trying to be nice enough, read the Bible enough, or be respectful enough won't fill the separation gap between us and God. Plus, all the trying so hard is super tiring.

But here's where the good news comes in: God sent His Son, Jesus, to live on earth and to die in your place so you can be forgiven for all your sins. When you trust in Jesus and begin a relationship with Him, you get to spend forever with God. And that starts immediately.

When you have a relationship with Jesus, you are forgiven. You don't have to worry about not being enough, because Jesus is. You don't have to stress over being strong, because Jesus is. And you don't have to live without God, ever, because He lives in you.

ANSWER
YOU CAN TRUST GOD.

ACTIVITY DAY

Now that you've finished all 100 days, let's go on a Scripture hunt! Flip back through this book, and look for Bible verses that have helped you the most. Then, open your Bible, search for those verses, and underline or highlight them. Don't want to write in your Bible? Put a sticky note or bookmark on those pages so that you can easily find them later. Use these verses as reminders of what's true and trustworthy when you're struggling with fear and worry!

ANSWER RECAP

- We know the Bible is true, which means heaven is too, and that is extremely exciting news.

- If anyone makes you feel like you don't matter, remember that you matter to God. You are unique and created for a purpose.

- Thank God that you have something to be excited about! Then ask Him to keep you focused on the day ahead.

- When things don't go as planned, look for the good. Remember that God always has a plan, and His plan is better than your own.

- Thankfully you have a God who specializes in taking your regret and giving you hope instead.

- God is not scared of the truth. He already knows what's going on, and He loves you no matter what.

- The Bible is our greatest resource to show us the proof that God is real.

- Pray as you go to bed. Talking to God will likely calm you down and help you fall asleep.

- The worry won't last forever, because God has already taken care of it. He wins, which means you do too.

- You can trust God.

INDEX

Use this index as a way to find a devotion written about something specific you're feeling or going through. Just look for that topic in the list to find which questions have to do with that subject!

ADOPTED Question 61

ALONE Question 13, Question 28, Question 72, Question 78

ANGER Question 40, Question 57, Question 77

ANNOYED Question 76

ANSWERS Question 84

ANTICIPATION Question 93

ANXIETY Question 12, Question 17, Question 18, Question 28, Question 30, Question 33, Question 46, Question 49, Question 51, Question 56, Question 59, Question 60, Question 67, Question 69, Question 71, Question 78

ARGUMENTS Question 40, Question 80

ASKING FOR HELP Question 39, Question 53

ASKING GOD FOR HELP Question 34, Question 42

BAD DAYS Question 65

BAD GRADES Question 63, Question 85

BAD NEWS Question 48

BEING A GOOD FRIEND Question 79

BEING STRONG Question 2

BELONGING Question 61

BIBLE STORIES Question 65

BIRTHDAY Question 92

BODY CHANGING Question 86

BORED Question 32

BRAVERY Question 70, Question 83

BROKEN BONES Question 2

BUSY Question 50

CALM Question 13

CHANGE Question 18, Question 28, Question 29, Question 62, Question 66, Question 86, Question 94

CHOSEN Question 61

COMPARISON Question 41, Question 52, Question 68

COMPASSION Question 6

CONFIDENCE Question 82, Question 89

CONFLICT Question 40, Question 81

CONFUSED Question 50, Question 83

CONTENT Question 32

COVID Question 94

CRIME Question 27

CRYING Question 47

CURIOSITY Question 1

DARKNESS Question 17

DENTIST Question 71

DISAGREEMENTS Question 80

DISAPPOINTED Question 76

DISTRACTED Question 13, Question 24, Question 36, Question 87, Question 98

DRAMA Question 40

DREAD Question 71

EMBARRASSMENT Question 9, Question 85

EMOTIONS Question 47, Question 77

EXCITED Question 38, Question 44, Question 93, Question 98

EXCLUDED Question 73

EXHAUSTED Question 98

EXPECTATIONS Question 22, Question 25, Question 52, Question 58

FAILURE Question 4, Question 6, Question 52

FAIRNESS Question 4, Question 6

FAITH Question 58

FAMILY Question 27, Question 61, Question 67

FEAR Question 3, Question 8, Question 10, Question 27, Question 49, Question 56

FEELING YOUNG Question 15, Question 37

FIRSTS Question 38

FITTING IN Question 41, Question 64

FOCUSING Question 87, Question 98

FORGIVENESS Question 26, Question 55, Question 96

FRIENDSHIP Question 9, Question 23, Question 31, Question 35, Question 64, Question 73, Question 79, Question 80, Question 89

FRUSTRATED Question 75, Question 85

GAME Question 78, Question 85

GOD HEARS Question 21

GRACE Question 55

GRADES Question 63

GUILT Question 55, Question 95

HARD DECISIONS Question 34, Question 83, Question 95

HARD SITUATION Question 97

HEALING Question 2

HEALTH Question 28

HEAVEN Question 91

HELP Question 8, Question 33, Question 34, Question 39, Question 42, Question 53

HOMESICK Question 74

HONEST Question 96

HOPE Question 16, Question 44, Question 48, Question 79, Question 95

HUMILITY Question 31

HURTING Question 23, Question 28, Question 57, Question 73

IDENTITY Question 15, Question 19, Question 29, Question 41, Question 61, Question 64, Question 68, Question 86, Question 89, Question 90, Question 92, Question 100

INDECISIVE Question 83, Question 88

INDEPENDENT Question 8

INSECURITY Question 19, Question 29, Question 35, Question 39, Question 41, Question 64, Question 68, Question 72, Question 89

INSIGNIFICANT Question 15, Question 37

JOBS Question 62, Question 67

JOY Question 79, Question 91, Question 93

KINDNESS Question 6

LAUGHTER Question 79

LEFT OUT Question 23, Question 37, Question 73

LONELY Question 23, Question 35, Question 72

LOSING Question 4, Question 6, Question 85

LOUD SURROUNDINGS Question 24

LYING Question 96

MAD Question 76

MAKING HARD DECISIONS Question 34, Question 83, Question 95

MEAN WORDS Question 92

MESSING UP Question 85, Question 63, Question 100

MISSING PEOPLE Question 74

MISTAKES Question 19, Question 26, Question 55, Question 85, Question 100

MOVING Question 28, Question 62, Question 70

NEEDING OTHERS Question 39

NERVOUS Question 7, Question 38, Question 46, Question 78, Question 79, Question 81

NEVER ALONE Question 74, Question 78, Question 88, Question 97

NEWS Question 10, Question 56

NIGHTMARE Question 14

NOT TIRED AND CAN'T SLEEP Question 36, Question 75

OBEDIENCE Question 43, Question 54, Question 90, Question 96

OUT OF YOUR CONTROL Question 12, Question 17, Question 18, Question 48, Question 49, Question 56, Question 58, Question 59, Question 60, Question 62, Question 66, Question 67, Question 76, Question 77

OVERSLEEPING Question 60

OVERWHELMED Question 8, Question 24, Question 25, Question 30, Question 33, Question 34, Question 42, Question 48, Question 50, Question 69, Question 87

PAIN Question 2, Question 28, Question 30

PARENTS Question 22

PATIENCE Question 20, Question 44

PEACE Question 13, Question 28, Question 69

PEER PRESSURE Question 43

PERFORMANCE Question 25

PRAYER Question 21, Question 27, Question 57, Question 69

PRESENTATION Question 78

PRESSURE TO MEASURE UP Question 41

PRIDE Question 22

PROTECTED Question 14, Question 50

PROVISION Question 29, Question 42, Question 59, Question 70, Question 83

PURPOSE Question 15, Question 20, Question 29, Question 37, Question 41, Question 45, Question 61, Question 90, Question 92, Question 94, Question 97

QUESTIONS Question 1, Question 11, Question 53, Question 84

REGRET Question 95

RESPECT Question 31

RESPONSIBILITY Question 63, Question 82

REST Question 32

RESTLESS Question 93

RESTORATION Question 91, Question 99

RULES Question 54

SADNESS Question 47, Question 74, Question 76

SAFETY Question 14, Question 28, Question 99

SCARED Question 3, Question 10, Question 13, Question 14, Question 17, Question 19, Question 27 Question 49, Question 67, Question 70, Question 81, Question 84, Question 99

SCHOOL Question 10, Question 51

SCHOOL DRILLS Question 49

SECURITY Question 88

SICKNESS Question 28

SOLO Question 78

SPORTS Question 4, Question 24, Question 52

STAND UP FOR WHAT IS RIGHT Question 90

STILLNESS Question 13

STORMS Question 10, Question 81

STRENGTH Question 2, Question 47, Question 83

STRESS Question 8, Question 18, Question 33, Question 36, Question 42, Question 50, Question 81

STRONG Question 2

TAKING TESTS Question 50, Question 51

TALKING TO GOD Question 21, Question 27, Question 57, Question 69

TEMPTATION Question 96

THANKFULNESS Question 29, Question 32, Question 98

THOUGHTS IN YOUR HEAD Question 87

TOUGHNESS Question 70

TRUST Question 5, Question 53, Question 54

TRYING REALLY HARD Question 100

UNANSWERED PRAYERS Question 45

UNDERSTOOD Question 21

UNEXPECTED Question 94

UNFAMILIAR PLACE Question 74

UNKNOWN Question 91

UNPREPARED Question 58

UNSURE Question 12, Question 18, Question 25, Question 83, Question 86

WAITING Question 12, Question 16, Question 20, Question 38, Question 44, Question 45

WEAKNESS Question 47

WISDOM Question 34

WORRY Question 7, Question 11, Question 16, Question 17, Question 25, Question 30, Question 33, Question 34, Question 45, Question 46, Question 49, Question 56, Question 58, Question 59, Question 60, Question 62, Question 66, Question 75, Question 79, Question 88, Question 99

THANK YOU

I knew I didn't want to write a single word of this book without hearing from boys and men in my life who could speak directly to the worries and fears they struggle with. I'm grateful my nephew, Blake, said yes to letting me pull his friends together so we could talk about the things no one really wants to talk about: *feelings*. Blake, his buddies, plus trusted guys in my life helped me make this book a resource that I pray will be useful for years to come.

So, to my Board of Bros: Blake, Conner, Landon, Hudson, Lucas, Knox, Andrew, Kyle, Adam, Sam, and Tony. Thank you for opening up and answering my questions! Your input led to all one hundred questions in this book, and I am so grateful for your help.

To my friends' boys: You may not be old enough to be on the Board of Bros yet, but this book is for you too. Beau, Will, Stetson, Wyn, Wilder, Asher, Everett, Wally, Arthur, Weston, Tucker, and Maverick . . . I cannot wait for you to read this one day!

To my people: Ansley, Caroline Flake, Erika, Lindsay, Tinsley, Dana, Caroline Green, Katie, Kelsey, Jayme, Erica, Elizabeth, Laura, Courtney, Stacey, Fern, Sarah, and Graham. The check-ins, cheers, and celebrations mean more than you will ever know. I'm a better human because of your friendship.

To my co-workers at IF:Gathering and Downs Books, Inc.: The ministry we've done together, the worked we've prayed over, the long hours we've laughed and cried through, have all grown me as a person and a follower of Jesus. Thank you for being some of my biggest supporters and encouragers, but mainly my friends. And Annie and Jennie, you've been longtime trusted voices in my life, but you are trusted voices to a lot of men and women around the world too. Your support of *You Can Rest* is a huge reason *You Can Trust* exists. You helped people know these resources are available, and I'm truly honored and grateful.

To my literary agent, Caroline Green: You're both my people and my agent, and I realize how much of a gift that is. Thank you for answering every text and call and being a cheerleader of both me and this book.

To my publishing team at B&H Kids: Devin Maddox, Michelle Freeman, Whitney Alexander: I am so grateful for your partnership, time, and expertise in this project. I respect you all so much!

To every coffee shop I wrote in: I feel like I owe you a shout-out. I do my best work surrounded by the buzz of my Nashville neighbors stopping in for their morning coffee or catching up with their friends at the table next to me. Here's to Starbucks (Hermitage), Eighth & Roast (West), Land of a Thousand Hills, Red Bicycle (Germantown & Woodbine), Ugly Mugs (East), Stay Golden, District Coffee, and Honest Coffee.

To my family: Mom, Dad, Clay, Connie, Ellie, Adam, Ansley, Shelby and Blake: Thank you for continuously being in my corner and being my built-in PR team. I love you very much!

And to my God: A lot of days I wondered if I was really supposed to be writing this book. You met me in that place every time and reminded me that You would provide. You would lead the way. You had this under control. It's as if you wanted me to relearn the very words I was writing: *I can trust You.*

Also available from
KATY BOATMAN

Preteen girls have lots to be anxious about, and Katy Boatman,
who has worked with them for 15 years, understands that. With an authentic
voice and mentor mindset, Katy wrote *You Can Rest* to help young readers calm
their hearts and minds by focusing on the one who brings true rest: Jesus.

Packed with grace and truth and sprinkled with humor and delight,
You Can Rest shows preteen girls that our worries and fears
do not have the final say. Jesus does.

AVAILABLE WHEREVER BOOKS ARE SOLD!